A Pillar of Fire to Follow

A Pillar of Fire to Follow
American Indian Dramas:
1808-1859

Priscilla Sears

Bowling Green University Popular Press
Bowling Green, Ohio 43403

To my family and Shelby Grantham and Laurence Davies

CONTENTS

Chapter I

"White is the highest color," pontificates Handsome Harry in *The Deerslayer*, "and therefore the best man; black comes next, and is put to live in the neighborhood of the white man, as tolerable and fit to be made use of; and red comes last, which shows that those what made 'em never expected an Indian to be accounted as more than half human."

Fenimore Cooper's character is artlessly racist, of course; but he is no less enmeshed in cultural myth than those of us who trust in the Western axiom that what is "really real" is quantifiable. In either case, the perceptions and evaluations are made according to myth[1]—by which I do not mean falsehood, though the word's common definition is "a traditional or legendary story usually concerning some superhuman being or some alleged person or event, with or without a determinable basis of fact or natural explanation." Here "myth" is used to describe those compelling complexes of images, symbols and stories which determine our sense of reality and divinity. We lay these psychological stencils over the data of the external world, which Robert Frost describes as "too much for the senses, / Too crowded, too confusing / Too present to imagine." These stencils determine not only what is included and what is omitted from our "too confusing, too crowded" ingestion, but also how what is admitted is configured: how the parts relate to one another. Myths not only determine what we perceive but also what the perceptions mean. They become a priori determinants of our individual and collective attitudes, judgments, beliefs and actions.

The widespread Judeo-Christian myth, for example, that animals are lower forms of life divinely intended for our use leads us to perceive them as separate and different from ourselves. This belief enables us to slaughter and eat them

1

without thanksgiving our indebtedness; sanctions our destruction of their habitats and food supplies; and allows us to torture them in the name of public entertainment. Contrastingly the Hopi Indians give thanks to the animal whose body is to be eaten:

> We say to the deer we are going to kill: We know your life is as precious as ours. We know that we are all one life on the same Mother Earth, beneath the same plains of the sky. But we also know that one life must give way to another so that the one great life of all may continue unbroken. So we ask your permission, we obtain your consent to the killing.
>
> Ceremoniously we said this... and it was proper so.... We built its flesh into our flesh; . . . and we knew that the life of the deer was continued in our life, and it in turn continued in the one life all around us, below us and above us....
>
> We are all bound together, and our touch upon one travels through all to return to us again.[2]

Some myths "travel through all," while others are discrete. Transcultural myths have been found in virtually the same form in many cultures, as Sir James Fraser has documented in *The Golden Bough*. There are universal conditions of human life and psychology that all cultures have in common, such as birth and death, the need for love, and what Richard Slotkin calls the "dream of an amenable universe."[3] The quest myth[4] and the sacred marriage of the divine king to the earth goddess or the spirit of place are universal, as is that of the retributive flood and the regeneration.

Other myths are cultural; that is, they occur widely and persistently in a culture and are stable centerpieces about which generations arrange themselves. They form the historical sense of a people, "reducing centuries of experience into a constellation of compelling metaphors" (Slotkin, p. 6), uniting them and guiding individual and collective behavior. For example, the frontier myth that made America a land of inexhaustible resources and opportunity for the self-reliant worker still colors our vision of reality, our attitude toward social reform, our exploration of space, and the conservation of our resources, and is reflected in our record of violence on the streets of home and in the jungles abroad.

Cultural myths underlie a culture's sense of what is real.

"Myth has a different meaning depending upon whether one speaks of other cultures or one's own. When we speak of others, a myth is [an untrue story].... When we speak of our own ... it suffices to ask 'What constitutes my culture's sense of reality?' "[5] When myths lose credibility in any culture and all that seemed fixed, dependable and "the way things are" becomes uncertain, arbitrary and unstable, the individuals of the society become susceptible to a debilitating and terrifying awareness of chaos and meaninglessness—what Michael Novak calls "an experience of nothingness." The world becomes "too present to imagine," and the culture is subject to disintegration.

Nietzsche predicted a nihilism and intoxication would result from the loss of the myth of the traditional Christian God: "intoxication with music, with cruelty, with hero-worship, with sex, with hatred; some sort of mysticism; art for art's sake, truth for truth's sake; narcotics against self-disgust; any silly, little fanaticism."[6] Joseph Campbell echoes Nietzsche. "With old mythologically founded taboos unsettled by our own modern science, there is everywhere in the civilized world a rapidly rising incidence of vice and crime, mental disorders, suicides and dope addictions, violence, murder, and despair."[7] Mythological instability was also characteristic of America during the first half of the nineteenth century when the Indian dramas analyzed in this study were written and performed.

Even when cultural myths are widely accepted, creating a stable psychological milieu, their validity as sources of information and as models for behavior varies. If myths remain unexamined and static while institutions, points of view and behavior in the nation or the world require change, they may have destructive and tragic effects. When myths allay social, political, economic or moral anxieties by providing simplistic solutions to complex problems, they are falsely reassuring and discourage more reliable and laborious methods of problem solving.

The myths that described America as the second Garden of Eden, a divinely appointed second chance for mankind, once had some basis in fact. The continent was a fabulous reality: vast, marvellously endowed, ostensibly without history, and, therefore, without sin, the "fresh green breast" in the presence of which "man must have held his breath" as Fitzgerald says in *The Great Gatsby*. It was a refuge for the disinherited, the oppressed, the persecuted and the defeated who migrated to begin again. As long as another frontier remained, there was still a chance to make a new start and maintain an idealistic American innocence, however qualified by Indian dispossession. But the time came when there were no more frontiers, no more territories for our Huck Finns to light out to, when the Civil War had exposed the national soul and when resources were diminished or exhausted. But the myth persisted, and it became evasion. As Thomas Merton points out, "Americans refused to see the flaming sword at their own door and continued to lay special claim to paradise and God's favor."[8]

Myths often, of course, do not remain static, but evolve and develop dramatically according to the psychological needs of a people in terms of their history and environment. The myth of Uncle Tom as a genial, self-sacrificing, accommodating, childish black man, looked after by an aristocratic, paternal and benevolent plantation owner reassured a nation espousing equality while condoning slavery. According to one myth, the black slaves were happy and pleased to sacrifice their lives and wills to superior beings who enlightened their darkness and treated them with justice and generosity.

Historical events also affect mythology. Francis Jennings points out that medieval theologians taught that the results of war could be legitimate only if the war was just. What whites call the "discovery" of the New World challenged this view. Since it was difficult to defend as righteous and defensive a war against an enemy who had never ventured within a thousand miles of one's domain, the old Crusades' myth that Holy Church's wars were automatically just was employed "to hallow the conquest of the New World."[9] This meant, of course, in Christian cosmology, that those conquered could be characterized not only as infidels but as demons. By the time of

King Philip's War in New England, 1672-74, a war fought between the Anglo-European settlers and a confederation of Wampanoag, Narragansett, Nipmuck, Abnaki and Mohawk Indians, the Puritan's errand in the wilderness had changed from redeeming the inhabitants to conquering them.[10] The few survivors of the burning of the Narragansett stronghold were typically described by Increase Mather as satanic: "When they came to see the ashes of their friends, mingled with the ashes of their fort... where the English had been doing a good day's work, they howl'd, they roar'd, they stamp'd, they tore their hair... and were the pictures of so many Devils in Desperation."[11] The savages were a sign of Satan's power. Their resistance to acculturation, including conversion, was infernal opposition to the divine. Warfare with "savages" suggested the earthly struggle against sin as well as Satanic plots against God's chosen,[12] or, as Lincoln said, "God's almost chosen."

The political circumstances that dominate the life of a people can also influence their mythic structures. Andrew Jackson's Removal Bill, passed and implemented during the 1830s, legalized the confiscation of Indian lands and forced the Indians to migrate to The Indian Territory in the West. The public outcry against the inhumanity and injustice of the bill was loud and long. The Supreme Court finally upheld the Indians' rights in a suit brought by the Cherokees, but President Jackson refused to implement the Court's ruling. It was during this period that many of the plays called "The Indian Dramas" were written and widely performed. They featured American Indian characters fighting with encroaching white settlers. A constant theme of these dramas is that the Indians must make way for the chosen people to realize their providentially appointed destiny.

Literature written by early colonists, particularly the journals, chronicles, promotional tracts, sermons and histories written by New Englanders of Puritan persuasion[13] influenced American national myths uniquely. The Colonies were founded in an age of printing, much of it done by the Puritans, who, as Slotkin points out, were much inclined toward the writing and printing of books and pamphlets and the creating of elaborate metaphors proving the righteousness of their proceedings. Since Americans turned readily to the printed word for the expression and the resolution of doubts, of problems of faith, of anxiety and aspiration, literature became the primary vehicle for the communication of mythic material, with the briefest of gaps between the inception of an oral legend and its being fixed in the public print. (Slotkin, p. 19)

This fixing of myths in print and in the public mind is explained by the mythogenesis theory of Richard Slotkin and Joseph Campbell. Myths, they contend, develop from a state of mind, a psychological readiness "to transform experience, perception, and narration into the materials of a myth... a process of reasoning-by-metaphor in which direct statement and logical analysis are replaced by figurative or poetic statement" (Slotkin, p. 7). This "reasoning-by-metaphor" is expressed by an individual artist to a receptive audience in the concrete form that Slotkin calls a "myth-artifact" (p. 8): the powerful story of associated images or symbols which command belief and which vary according to the culture and the times. Hereafter in this study, "myth" will be used in this sense of "myth-artifact."

In colonial America, the state of readiness to "reason by metaphor" was induced by the abrupt transition from a familiar environment and history, in which old myths structured experience satisfactorily, to a strange, wild environment, in which the mythological heritage could not always deal with the peculiar needs and conditions of the New World. After the Revolutionary War, the need for stories identifying and explaining national experience and destiny was expressed in part as an urgent call for an American literature. Patriots with literary inclinations, from the first Comptroller of the Treasury, James Barker, to veterans of Pontiac's Siege of Detroit, such as Alexander Macomb, responded. They often imitated one another and established mythic formulas and conventions that became "a sort of given between writer and audience, a set of tacit assumptions on the nature of human experience, on human and divine motivations, on moral values, and on the nature of reality" (Slotkin, p. 20).

Similarly, after the War of 1812 and throughout the first half of the nineteenth century, writers were asked to provide an American literature that provoked "a cry in the blood"[14]—that is, an American mythology, dramatizing the American situation in American terms, and unifying the nation. "Give me but the writing of the national ballads and I care not who has the framing of the laws," wrote the playwright Robert Dale Owen.[15]

Thus American literature became both a creator of myth-artifact in the sense of literary conventions that inspired belief, and also a vehicle for the transmission of myths. This meant, of course, that those factors that influence literature also affected our cultural myths. The myths were, for example, subject to the fluctuations of the literary marketplace. The writers, moreover, often had to deal with materials such as the frontier, the Indians, or historical events with which they had neither first-hand experience nor reliable sources, and which had to be modified according to artistic needs and audience preferences.

Literature was not the only conveyor of myths, of course. Other institutions of culture—the government, the church, the family, the industries and the schools—also contributed. During the first half of the nineteenth century, the American longing for national identity was intense, and the myth of America as a new beginning and of Americans as instruments of God, "emancipated from history, happily bereft of ancestry.... Undefiled by... family and race... self-reliant... fundamentally innocent,"[16] and as exemplars for the rest of the world was being promulgated in all institutions. "Our national birth," declaimed the *Democratic Review* in 1839, "was the beginning of a new history... which separates us from the past and connects us with the future only" (p. 5). The most widely used elementary school reading text throughout this time, William H. McGuffey's *Eclectic Reader*, instructed its students that the United States "holds out an example... to those nine-tenths of the human race who are born without heredity, rank

or fortune," and demonstrates "that it is practicable to elevate
the mass of mankind... to raise them to self-respect."[17] In 1832,
Daniel Webster, speaking in Worcester, Massachusetts, said:
"In our endeavor to maintain our existing form of government,
we are not acting for ourselves alone, but for the whole globe.
We are trustees holding a sacred treasure, in which all lovers of
freedom have a stake.... The gaze of the sons of liberty
everywhere is upon us, anxiously, intently, upon us" (Nye, p.
173). Orestes Brownson, a Unitarian minister, who later
became a reactionary editor of Roman Catholic magazines,
predicted that we would succeed in executing our "divine
orders" to realize the natural rights of man in society and in
fulfilling mankind's hopes "...if we return to God, put our trust
in Him, and live for the end of which He has appointed us."[18]
James Fenimore Cooper was writing about the godly, young,
innocent Natty Bumppo, a self-reliant, seemingly orphaned,
spiritual hero, in love with God and Nature, living free of time
and restraints.

This study has a dual purpose: first to describe the myths
about the Native Americans and Anglo-Europeans that
appear in the Indian Dramas, melodramas written 1808-1858,
and to appraise their validity; second to identify the
psychological needs and historical forces that determined their
character.

The Indian Dramas feature Indian characters in plots
centered on Indian-white relationships, as seen by American
writers. They are valuable cultural documents, containing all
the major myths about native Americans in our literature and
life. They are also clear manifestations of the contemporary
American psyche and situation, crystallizing preoccupations
of the nineteenth century and revealing meanings which have
been masked because of fear, guilt and rage.

These "national dramas" flourished during the 1830s,
after John Augustus Stone's *Metamora or The Last of the*
Wampanoags (1829) **gained unprecedented commercial
success and established a literary formula that was widely
imitated. The formula set up between audience and writer (and**

other writers) a relationship of givens about the characters of red and white and the state of their societies. Arthur Hobson Quinn, in *A History of the American Drama*, estimates that thirty-five plays like *Metamora* were written in twenty years.[19] During that time, novels about Indians were also dramatized. Robert Montgomery Bird's *Nick of the Woods* was adapted into sentimental melodrama, and James Fenimore Cooper's *The Wept of Wish-ton-Wish* was anonymously dramatized and performed in all the important theaters in the country.[20] These dramatized myths satisfied psychological needs in a form appropriate to Americans' historical and physical experience through the first half of the nineteenth century.

Such popular plays deeply affected the understanding, attitudes and behavior of Americans toward "our Indians" and ourselves. Indeed, myths from these plays persist in our literature, still directing our relations with the Indians, since no new, more valid myths have arisen to replace or modify them. The only additions have been myths of the oil-rich Indian and the vanished American, sequel to the nineteenth century's vanishing American.

The plays have not received the scholarly attention they deserve. Quinn touches briefly upon the historically outstanding plays, from *Ponteach*, by Robert Rogers (1776), to *Hiawatha*, by John Brougham (1856). Montrose Moses, in *The American Dramatist*[21] examines several typical plays from this group to illustrate the misrepresentation of the Indian as a white man with a savage heart. Eight American dramas are analyzed by Roy Harvey Pearce. He studies them as cultural documents that express the American idea of savagery as it conflicted with the European literary and philosophic tradition of the noble savage. In *The Indian in American Literature*, Albert Keiser considers the mythology of the Indian from Captain John Smith's Pocahantas legend in *The Generall Historie of Virginia, New England and the Summer Isles* (1624) to Hamlin Garland's works in the 1920s. His analysis of the accuracy of the myths rests on the usual assumptions:[22] that the Indians are of one race and one culture, that they are inferior to Anglo-European culture, that the "hardy pioneers" of this virile white race had to treat the **"terrible Blackfeet," the "untamed Pawnees" and their** "mongrel offspring" as they did, that the injustice of the treatment afforded the Indian is only apparent, and that the portrayal of the native Americans as aliens in Francis Parkman's *The Conspiracy of Pontiac* is "an admirable one." Keiser concludes with a final stereotype, that of the twentieth-century Indian as debauched primitive "rolling in wealth produced by the oil gushers of Oklahoma." He suggests that the Indian is reaping a golden harvest and that the "child of nature," adapting to "new-found freedom" and wealth, will not become integrated into white civilization. Robert J. Berkhofer, Jr., in *The White Man's Indian: Images of the American Indian from Columbus to the Present*, does exemplify and explicate the myths and images of Indians in non-dramatic literature and art, philosophy and science, seeing in them recurrent efforts of whites to understand and criticize white values and ideas, but he fails to include the Indian dramas.

Many of these unexamined works are, moreover, threatened with extinction. Fewer than half of the forty Indian dramas written after 1820 and before 1860 are extant, and many of these exist in single copies so fragile that they cannot be microfilmed. All but three of those remaining are included in this study.

In the second chapter I have described the few actual common cultural and physical traits of the diverse tribes of American Indians, traits which contrast markedly with their counterparts in the plays. This chapter also characterizes contemporary intercultural relationships which influenced the myths expressed by the plays. Chapters III and IV analyze the plays themselves, identifying the myths and documenting the way they sanitized genocidal realities. Chapter V analyzes the contemporary American situation and psychology, which are both manifested in and treated by the Indian dramas.

This study is intended to contribute to the liberation of the native American from the prison of debilitating myths and images which have become fixed in American literature and life. It should also contribute to the critical awareness of pervasive myths which have figured in the suppression of facts and the evasion of moral issues in our national life. Finally, this book is a response to Frank Waters' novel *The Man Who Killed the Deer*, in which the Hopis ask: "What have we done to our brother? What have we done to ourselves? For we all are bound together, and our touch upon one travels through all to return to us again."

Chapter 2

[As part of a 1744 treaty between the Indians of the Six Nations and the colonies of Virginia and Maryland, the Indians were invited to send boys to William and Mary College. They declined, saying:] We know that you highly esteem the kind of learning taught in those colleges, and that the maintenance of our young men, while with you, would be very expensive to you. We are convinced that you mean to do us good by your proposal; and we thank you heartily. But, you, who are wise, must know that different Nations have different conceptions of things and you will therefore not take this amiss, if our ideas of this kind of education happen not to be the same as yours. We have had some experience of it. Several of our young people were formerly brought up at the Colleges of the Northern Provinces; they were instructed in all your Sciences; but, when they came back to us, they were bad runners, ignorant of every means of living in the woods... neither fit for hunters, warriors, nor counsellors, they were totally good for nothing. We are, however, not the less oblig'd by your kind offer, tho' we decline accepting it; and, to show our grateful sense of it, if the Gentlemen of Virginia would send us a dozen of their sons, we will take care of their education, instruct them in all we know, and make men of them.

Samuel J. Drake, *Biography and History*
of the Indians of North America,
Third Edition (Boston: O.L. Perkins
and Hillard, Gray and Co., 1835), p. 27.

"The animals vulgarly called Indians"[1] are depersonalized and dehumanized symbols in American life. "The Indian is a savage." "The Indian is a drunk." "The Indian squaw has no shame." "The Indian princess is a forest fawn." "The Indian is a forest King." "The only good Indian is a dead Indian."[2] These familiar cliches and the attitudes they represent have roots in historical utterances typified in nineteenth-century Indian Dramas. In American literature at large, the Indian is narrowly characterized in four distinct and undeviating ways, having been reduced to a manageable simplicity, a set of embalming stereotypes.

Most of the Indian dramas lay claim to historical and biographical accuracy, or at least to sources of "unimpeachable testimony."[3] But, in fact, they do not truly represent the diverse character of the Indian peoples. Moreover, they are not uniformly veracious in their descriptions of the encounters and the personalities dramatized. **They distort historical sources and rely on** spurious "testimonies."[4] In some instances, these alterations of history were prompted by artistic requirements. For example, the actual sequence of events was sometimes rearranged to provide more intense dramatic development, as in Custis' *Pocahontas*. The action had to be limited to the stage, of course, and major figures in the historical conflict were frequently omitted to avoid distracting subplots. The dearth of anthropological information and the absence of objective histories of tribes before and after contact with the whites also limited fidelity to fact.[5]

The general ignorance about Native Americans had led to ambivalence, uncertainty and confusion from the time of the earliest contacts, which became more intense, of course, with increasing colonization. To relieve their anxiety about the unknown, to develop a way of processing the flood of new phenomena, and to defend their sense of themselves (as God's chosen, in the case of the Puritans), the colonists quickly adapted the romantic and conventional European noble savage myths to the American experience (Berkhofer, pp. 3-25). These adaptations relieved the collective insecurity, anxiety and guilt by providing order and structure. This mythological legacy, revised in accord with colonial needs, also partially satisfied those needs generated by the Anglo-European-Native American interaction of the period during which the plays were written.

Despite their self-proclaimed historical and biographical accuracy, the dramas are, in fact, misrepresentations and distortions. Their stories are based on information and assumptions as invalid as the name "Indians." The native peoples, for instance, were not all the same. They did not all look alike nor think alike, nor did they share a sense of common identity. There were vast racial, linguistic, cultural and mythological differences. The few common characteristics that did exist, moreover, did not figure importantly in their literary characterization. Individual native people, leaders such as Tecumseh, Metacomet and Pontiac, are often misrepresented as merely ambitious and indiscriminately warlike. Battles, which are always the form given to red-white encounters outside the Pocahontas plays, are also inaccurately depicted.

The first step toward substantiating the discrepancy between myths and actuality in these plays requires a brief account of the few cultural traits common to the hundreds of different Indian tribes. Clarification of the red-white intercultural circumstances of the period when the plays were written is also important in explaining the discrepancy, and it is necessary to review the Indian affairs which preoccupied white America during the first half of the nineteenth-century, noting the contrasts between putative history and the actualities as we know them.

When Columbus "discovered" the Western Hemisphere, an estimated fourteen million Native Americans lived in the area that is now the continental United States.[6] They were organized into hundreds of societies or tribes, speaking about three hundred languages, and had they met, they would have found each other mutually unintelligible in language, religion and culture. Wars were frequent among neighboring tribes such as the Narragansetts, Wampanoags and Pequots of New England, and animosity was traditional. Before the white invasion, the native people had no sense of collective racial or cultural identity.

The fundamental intertribal differences were many and varied. Some tribes, such as the Cheyenne, were hunting societies; others, like the Hopis and other Pueblo groups, were agricultural societies; the Apache and Navajo were essentially warrior societies. Some tribes reckoned descent by the father, some by the mother. The Iroquois regarded vengeance as a **religious duty; the Hopi abhorred violence against any** on the earth. As there was no "Indian language," no "Indian **character," and no "Indian religion," there was no pure radical** strain. "Red" skin varied from a light yellow to a copper color.

Plains people were tall, the men essentially beardless and lean; Indians of California were rotund, short and the men heavily bearded. There was also wide tribal variation in size and eye structure. Only after contact with whites resulted in common diseases, demoralizations and degradations were leaders like Metacomet (called King Philip by the colonists), Tecumseh and Pontiac able to unite, however briefly, the diverse tribes in the common cause of repelling the invader. Tecumseh, or Shooting Star, a celebrated Shawnee war chief, organized a short-lived Indian confederation early in the nineteenth century to resist the constant white encroachment. He said:

> The Being within, communing with past ages, tells me that once... there was no Whiteman on this continent, that it then all belonged to the Great Spirit that made the Redman to keep it, to traverse it, to enjoy its productions, and to fill it with the same race, once a happy race; since made miserable by the White people, who are never contented but always encroaching.
> The way, and the only way, to check and to stop this evil is for all the Redmen to unite in claiming a common and equal right to the land, as it was at first and should be yet; for it was never divided, but belongs to all for the use of each (Drake, pp. 100-101).

Yet, even before the redmen recognized their common plight, tribes from the woodlands, the plains, the mountains, deserts and coasts did share a few fundamental traits that were, au fond, antipathetic to the religious and cultural heritage of the Puritans and their physical and cultural heirs.[7]

The Native Americans' image of themselves was static, as Frederick Turner points out.[8] They did not conceive of themselves as penitent marchers in a parade to the millennium as the Puritans did; they did not seek or welcome change and progress. Crazy Horse, the mystic warrior of the Oglala Sioux, spoke for all when he said: "We would live as our fathers did and their fathers before them." The past was a sacred trust. "To us the ashes of our ancestors are sacred," said Chief Seattle of the Dwamesh, "and their resting place is hallowed ground."[9] Chief Joseph, leader of the Nez Perce, responding to the whites' divisions of the land into surveyed lots and the cultivating of those lots, said: "The earth... should be left as it was.... The country was made without lines of demarcation, and it is no man's business to divide it."[10]

In general, the native Americans saw themselves neither as cultivators improving their lots nor as fearful antagonists of a hostile environment. Instead they imagined themselves as participants in the huge and sacred cycle of life, interdependent with all other parts:

We did not think of the great open plains, the beautiful rolling hills, and winding streams with tangled growth, as 'wild.' Only to the white man was nature a wilderness and only to him was the land 'infested' with 'wild animals' and 'savage' people. To us it was tame. Earth was bountiful and we were surrounded with the blessings of the Great Mystery. Not until the hairy man from the east came and with brutal frenzy heaped injustices upon us and the families we loved was it 'wild' for us. When the very animals of the forest began fleeing from his approach, then it was that for us the 'Wild West' began.[11]

Chief Luther Standing Bear of the Oglala Sioux, who had been educated at the Indian school at Carlisle, Pennsylvania, spoke of the sense of kinship the Indian had with all creation— a partnership in the cosmic life. This world view and self view differed from the prevailing white theology, which set the natural in opposition to the spiritual. Living in the world was not thought of as a punishment by the Indians, as it was, at least in part, by the Puritans:

The Lakota was a true naturist—a lover of nature. He loved the earth and all things of the earth, the attachment growing with age. The old people came literally to love the soil, and they sat or reclined on the ground with a feeling of being close to a mothering power. It was good for the skin to touch the earth and the old people liked to remove their mocassins and walk with bare feet on the sacred earth. Their tipis were built upon the earth and altars were made of earth. The birds that flew in the air came to rest upon the earth and it was the final abiding place of all things that lived and grew. The soil was soothing, strengthening, cleansing, and healing.

That is why the old Indian still sits upon the earth instead of propping himself up and away from its life-giving forces. For him, to sit or lie upon the ground is to be able to think more deeply and to feel more keenly; he can see more clearly into the mysteries of life and come closer in kinship to other lives about him....

Kinship with all creatures of the earth, sky and water was a real and active principle. For the animal and bird world there existed a brotherly feeling that kept the Lakota safe among them and so close did some Lakotas come to their feathered and furred friends that in true brotherhood they spoke a common tongue.

The old Lakota was wise. He knew that man's heart away from nature becomes hard; he knew that lack of respect for growing, living things soon led to lack of respect for humans too. So he kept his youth close to its softening influence.

Chief Luther Standing Bear,
Land of the Spotted Eagle
(Boston: Houghton Mifflin, 1911), p. 192.

The Indian was not only nature's inhabitant who wore it **"easily and gracefully," as Henry David Thoreau observed in** *Walden*, but he was also an organic part of it, living tissue of its body that was sustained by the symbiotic functioning of all parts.

The Indian believes he is a cannibal.... All of his life he must eat his brothers and sisters and deer and corn which is the mother, and the fish which is the brother. All our lives we must eat off them and be a cannibal, but when we die we give back all that we have eaten, and our body goes to feed the worms that feed the birds. And it feeds the roots so that the trees and the grass grow so that the deer can eat it and the birds can nest in the tree. And we can give back. (Armstrong and Turner, p. 160).

John Collier, Commissioner of Indian Affairs from 1933 to 1945, saw this reverence and passion for the earth and the "web of life" ramifying into a reverence and passion for the individual human personality. This was expressed in a love of personal freedom and hatred of restraint that Anglo-Europeans often misinterpreted as anarchy, lawlessness, economic backwardness, and later as Jacobinic excess (Collier, p. 16). Indian society was, in fact, regulated by customs rather than laws, and these accommodated individualism remarkably well. Among the Cheyenne, for instance, decisions made by the governing council had to be unanimous.[12] Divorce was a profound but personal matter. Jails were unknown.[13] In general, no authority was hereditary. Chiefs were elected and their powers limited (Slotkin, p. 44); priests were consultative, not magisterial. As Richard Slotkin observes, the problem of government was not the Anglo-European sort of conflict of contending authorities, as between the state and the church, but the matter of authority itself. How could essentially free men fulfill the organic need to join together for survival? What was the "fecund minimum" required?

The need was certainly real. The Indians' world was not a secure one: wars, floods, pestilence, drought and storms threatened existence. Indians lived dangerously and their survival was contingent upon group membership. This need and that of personal freedom were reconciled in societies that were free and open, accommodating and nurturing the individual while also inspiring a sense of kinship that transcended the understanding of the rationally self-interested person. Tribal membership was not contingent upon being one of the elect: you belonged in the same way as all members because you were born into the society. The survival of the group was thought to depend upon the rendering of individual services and upon the development of intense and self-willed personalities,[14] who could, in partnership with the gods and in cooperation with the society, prosperously co-exist with nature. In turn, the tribe provided for all its members, generally without reference to individual contribution. The elderly, the orphaned, the widowed, and other "helpless ones" were supported. Liberal and reciprocal generosity to kinspeople and the community was a functional necessity and mark of greatness.[15] Montaigne, in his *Essays* (Chapter 30, Book I), wrote of "the new world we have lately discovered" and of "the Caniballes." He had learned of the Indians by reading travel ooks, talking with explorers, and interviewing several Indians who were brought to France during the reign of Charles IX (1560-1574). He commented on what he interpreted as their classless communal life:

They had perceived there were men amongst us full gorged with all sorts of commodities, and others which were hunger-starved and bare with need and povertie, begged at their gates: and found it strange that these people so needy could endure such an injustice, and that they took not the others by the throte, or set fire on their house....

Among the "caniballes," when one starved, they all starved.[16]

This sense of community was also evident in the Native American concept of property, which was different from

European concepts, and the difference often produced confict. As Wilcomb Washburn points out, "In general, there was a greater emphasis by Indians on user's rights and less emphasis on the rights and power of nominal owners, whether those nominal owners were individuals or the tribe" (p. 32). For example, the nominal owner could not violate usufructory rights by preventing use or arbitrary disposal, unless such action was taken in keeping with tribal custom. Moreover, as Fey and MacNickle observe, the Native Americans did not understand giving the right of permanent possession of the soil nor the European concept of the merchantability of land. Although tribal domains were recognized and respected, there were no formal, recorded titles to the land.

There were humane, social and agricultural reasons for these sharing patterns. In 1881, Congress considered a bill to force Indian tribes to divide their tribal lands among individuals. The Five Civilized Tribes, so-called because they were the most acculturated, petitioned Congress to allow them to continue as they were:

Our people have not asked for or authorized this, for the reason that they believe it could do no good and would only result in mischief in their present condition. Our own laws regulate the system of land tenure suited to our condition, and much safer than that which is proposed for it.

Improvements can be and frequently are sold, but the land itself is not a chattel. Its occupancy and possession are indispensable to holding it, and its abandonment for two years makes it revert to the public domain. In this way every one of our citizens is assured of a home. The change to individual title would throw the whole domain in a few years into the hands of a few persons.

A large portion of our country, and at least two-thirds of the Indian country, are only suitable for grazing purposes. No man can afford to live by stock raising and herding who is restricted to 160 or even 320 acres, especially on lands away from water.[17]

The Reverend John Heckewelder, the Moravian missionary who lived with and wrote about the Delawares during the late eighteenth and early nineteenth centuries, and whose work was one of James Fenimore Cooper's primary sources, wrote of the spiritual Indian attitude toward the land and its products:

Not satisfied with paying this first of duties to the Lord of all, in the best manner they are able, the Indians also endeavor to fulfill the views which they suppose he had in creating the world. They think that he made the earth and all that it contains for the common good of all mankind; when he stocked the country that he gave them with plenty of game, it was not for the benefit of a few, but of all. Every thing was given in common to the sons of men. Whatever liveth on the land, whatsoever groweth out of the earth, and all that is in the rivers and waters flowing through the same, was given jointly to all, and every one is entitled to his share. From this principle, hospitality flows as from its source. With them it is not a virtue but a strict duty. Hence they are never in search of excuses to avoid giving, but freely supply their neighbor's wants from the stock prepared for their own use. They give and are hospitable to all, without exception, and will always share with each other and often with the stranger, even to their last morsel. They rather would lie down themselves on an empty stomach, than have it laid to their charge that they had neglected their duty, by not satisfying the wants of a stranger, the sick or the needy. The stranger has a claim to their hospitality, partly on account of his being at a distance from his family and friends, and partly because he has honoured them by his visit, and ought to leave them with a good impression upon his mind; the sick and the poor because they have a right to be helped out of the common stock: for the meat they have been served was taken from the woods, it was common before the hunter took it; if corn or vegetables, it had grown out of the common ground, yet not by the power of the man, but by that of the Great Spirit. Besides, on the principle that all are descended from one parent, they look upon themselves as but one great family, who therefore ought at all times and all occasions, to be serviceable and kind to each other, and by that means make themselves acceptable to the head of the universal family, the great and good Mannitto.[18]

The idea that the earth and "the fullness thereof" was provided for all made the Native American especially vulnerable to the land-hungry Anglo-Europeans, who, Roger Williams feared, would fall into the idolatry of land worship.[19] The compliance of Native Americans with the early settlers' lust for land simply whetted the appetite of Europeans who believed in the absolute power of the nominal owner of land, and who associated land ownership with political and religious freedom.

Later Native Americans were disabused and realized that the tide of white immigration and avarice could not be stemmed or satisfied and that the contractual deeding of land was not only permanent, but prevented them from using the land for hunting or farming and even from moving on it. Thereafter there was widespread resistance to efforts to buy or take their lands. When a northern Blackfoot chief was asked for his signature on one of the first land treaties in his region (the Milk River, near the northern border of Montana and the Northwest Territories) he responded:

Our land is more valuable than your money. It will last forever. It will not even perish by the flames of fire. As long as the sun shines and the waters flow, this land will be here to give life to men and animals; therefore we cannot sell it because it does not belong to us. You can count your money and burn it within the nod of a buffalo's head, but only the Great Spirit can count the grains of sand and the blades of grass of these plains. As a present to you, we will give you anything that we have that you can take with you; but the land, never.[20]

Subsequently, the federal and local governments often secured Native American lands either by appointing local chiefs who were willing to sign deeds for favors or by accepting the signature of the leader or leaders of one or several bands of a tribe as legally binding upon all members. The agreement of the Creeks to cede fifteen million acres in the Southeast to the state of Georgia is a case in point. William MacIntosh, cousin of the Governor of Georgia, and twelve Creek chiefs signed the treaty. Thirty-six others, representing nine-tenths of the tribe, refused to sign.

Simple wants, cooperative labor, and patterns of sharing enabled the Indians to live relatively leisurely lives. They could not understand why the whites thought they should work all year when they could supply their collective wants in six months and devote the rest of the year to such things as meditating, fasting, rituals, dancing, playing games and fashioning art works. "Indolent" was the word the New England colonists used most often to describe the Native Americans.[21] Indolence was, of course, not only incomprehensible but sacrilegious to those who created the American work ethic, which Max Weber described as "the earning of more and more money, combined with the strict avoidance of all spontaneous enjoyment of life, which led to gain, profit, and acquisition."

The Indians' failure to assign primal sanctity to property and their supposed nomadic, hunting style of life were thought to be significant deterrents to civilizing them.[22] Henry Knox, Secretary of War under Washington, observed: "Were it possible to introduce among the Indian tribes a love for exclusive property, it would be a happy commencement of the business of civilizing them" (Armstrong and Turner, p. xxi).

The other means of transforming the Native American from a "rude savage" into a refined, civilized citizen was to be religious conversion. Yet fundamental differences of opinion about theology, cosmology, genesis and human nature retarded conversion, and while the seventeenth century saw some early successes by New England missionaries like John Eliot and Samuel Gookins, as well as the Pennsylvania Quakers on the frontier and the Catholics in northern New England and Florida and Georgia, the conversion rate soon fell off.[23] Many ethical similarities between the cultures, such as prohibitions against lying and stealing and murder, had been helpful. But among Native Americans, these were often matters of social custom and natural law, which they believed to be moral law, rather than of divine decree expressed in written civil and religious laws.[24] David Thompson, writing about his life among the Indians as he traveled in the West from 1784 through 1812 observed: "The morality of the Indians may be said to be founded on its necessity to the peace and safety of each other, although they profess to believe in a spirit of great power...."[25] John Collier, writing about the Indians of California and the Plains, observed:

They say... that men must follow the right path of living. They must live according to the laws of nature which are moral laws. If they fail to do that, they hurt themselves and that is all the punishment there is. They point to the Milky Way which is a path across heaven, but which has a branch leading off into emptiness. If a man fails to live according to the laws of nature, he goes off that side branch which ends in emptiness.[26]

Ethnocentric European observers often assumed that the absence of a written code of laws and European religious and judicial institutions meant that the Indians had no concept of justice and law and no systematic control of behavior. Moreover, the Native American insistence on private retributive justice, which Washburn argues was not only an expression of individual personality but also of a socio-political system (p. 20), was regarded by whites as demonic. Other practices used to establish proper relationships with the supernatural world, such as vision quests, withdrawal experiences, harvest rituals, purification ceremonies and self-torture, were interpreted as shameless irreverence, or, worse, devil worship.

The plurality and character of some Native American deities was also considered diabolical. The Native American spirit world was populated by varied beings and powers who were believed to influence human and animal actions. Two constrasting spiritual forces were common, one beneficent and the other principally malevolent. Two such contrasting figures among Eastern tribes were the supreme being called the Master of Breath and the archetypal Great Rabbit, a mischief-maker, obscene by European standards, who played jokes and made trouble, like Pau-Puk-Keewis in Longfellow's "The Song of Hiawatha." The former tended to be remote, abstract and transcendental, while the latter was often personal and immanent. Many of the deities of the traditional Navajo religion, for example, were, like pre-Christian Greek gods, surprisingly human. They became angry and jealous; they experienced fear; they could be ritually coerced into submitting to mortal will; they made love; they defecated.

Two other constants in the Indian pantheon were the powerful, creative, sexually-related maternal and paternal deities. The maternal deity not only was of the earth, she was the earth itself. By her coition with the paternal deity, associated with spirit, action and energy, all was created. These universal parents were often referred to as Mother Earth and Father Sky. Contrastingly, the Puritan myth acknowledged but one God, who was just, transcendent, asexual, omnipotent, inscrutable and rigorous as well as merciful and loving. He was related to humanity in a remote and uncertain way. Jehovah could not be coerced or moved by any form of human behavior, even by the works of the pious and holy. All people were tainted by the original sin of rebellion against authority. Living in the world was a punishment for that sin, although it was also an opportunity to repent and to gain a new spiritual self by self-abasement and obedience to God's will as expressed in his scriptures.

The two cultures' myths about genesis were also contradistinctive, resulting in diametrically opposed conceptions of the natural world and humanity's relationship with it. The Delawares' myth of genesis is typical. In the beginnning, people lived miserably in an underwater darkness. Relief came when the hero of the tribe pursued a deer through a hole and came through into this world in a forest. He skillfully tracked the deer, killed it and ate it. As he did so, he had a vision of the beauty and goodness of his Mother, the Earth. When his people ate the flesh of the deer, they too were awakened and followed the hero out of the underworld into a better place, where they could enjoy and worship the kind, maternal goddess (Slotkin, p. 46). Instead of being expelled from a providential garden where all wants were supplied, and driven apart from God into the howling and barren wilderness to despair and repent, they were admitted to a wonderful place, a sacred place, by the confident action of an exemplary mortal, inspired by natural impulses. They were not enjoined to repress and abase their natural and sinful selves in order to extirpate evil, or solemnly and rationally to worship an inhuman God partly by strict obedience and passivity. Indians believed they were expected to express their natural selves actively and intuitively in joy and thanksgiving for their deliverance through the agency of the individual people and Mother Earth. They worshipped the world just as it was: the good and the bad, the threatening and the comforting. Nature was revered, not despised and feared. Man was in partnership with the divine, kin to all life and gods and the earth, not a vile, weak, ignorant creature who might hope to repent in dust and ashes.

The ways were past mutual understanding. "Our religion seems foolish to you," said Sitting Bull, "but so does yours to me" (Armstrong and Turner, p. 128). At the end of a dialogue between the Seneca Chief Red Jacket and a Boston missionary, the Chief observed that God had made great differences between His red and white children; it was possible that in His infinite wisdom, he had assigned them different religions. The

Chief then offered to shake hands, but the missionary backed away and replied that he could not, that there was no fellowship between the religion of God and the works of the devil.[27]

*   *   *

As the Indians who declined to send their young men to William and Mary observed, "different nations have different conceptions of living." The mythologically-inspired differences between the red and white cultures were profound. Although Native Americans were far more culturally diverse than their conquerors,[28] a few intertribal similarities existed. They shared a common concept of the self as an individual and a member of society, and of the relationship of that self with the world and with God.

Native Americans saw themselves as distinct individuals, proud and free, but also as vital, interdependent parts of the sacred cycle of the life of all time, and as charged with the preservation of the traditional culture. They labored cooperatively in what was primarily a classless society, in which vested authority was limited, the sharing ethic was the rule, and individual human rights were accorded precedence over property rights. Their spirituality was profound and pervasive. Their gods varied in character and power, but their relationships with them were usually personal and achieved through intuition and dreams, as well as prayers and tribal ritual. For the most part these gods were more human, more involved in the world, more susceptible to human influence, and more tolerant than the Judeo-Christian deity.

Early nineteenth-century Anglo-American consciousness of Native Americans was dominated by conceptual contrasts and by intercultural conflicts. The white man was not interested in the Native American as a partner in an intercultural national enterprise, but as the identifying other: what the white man was not and could not be. The tragic results for Indians of interracial contact suggested to the victorious Anglo-European, however, an abhorrent vision of himself as cruel, perfidious and unjust. National character of this flavor was intolerable, of course. Soothing myths which justified the dispossession and destruction of Native Americans as an inevitable consequence of spreading civilization became very popular. Thomas Farnham, writing in 1843 about the fate of the Sauks and the Foxes, observed: "like all tribes.... they also dwindle away at the approach of the whites. A melancholy fact. The Indians' bones must enrich the soil before the plough of the civilized man can open it."[29]

The red people "dwindled" rapidly. They were being moved from their ancestral homes by fraud and direct military action. Their characters were being dissolved in bootlegged liquor. They were subjected to the white frontiersmen's cruelty. The missionaries' frantic efforts to Christianize them were failing. Tribe after tribe was becoming extinct. They were the vanishing American (Pearce, p. 74).

These "melancholy reflections," as Andrew Jackson called them, excited much public outrage, especially among non-frontier Americans. Ralph Waldon Emerson's letter to President Van Buren about the removal of the Cherokee to the Indian Territory in 1838 expressed a common reaction:

[This removal is] a dereliction of all faith and virtue,.. a denial of justice, and... a deafness to screams of mercy never heard of in times of peace and the dealing of a nation with its own allies and wards, since the earth was made. Sir, does this government think that the people of the United States are become savage and mad? From their mind are the sentiments of love and a good nature wiped clean out? The soul of man, the justice, the mercy, that is the heart's heart in all men, from Maine to Georgia, does abhor this business.... A crime is projected that really deprives us as well as the Cherokees of a country for how could we call the conspiracy that should crush these poor Indians our government, or the land that was cursed by their parting and dying imprecations our country, any more?[30]

The Cherokee Removal to which Emerson refers was the best known and most spectacular case of the period, and it exemplified the official treatment afforded the Native American by state and federal governments. The Cherokees comprised the largest of the Five Civilized Tribes. (This group also included the Choctaw, Chickasaw, Creek and Seminole nations.) They inhabited the southern Alleghenies, from eastern Tennessee into the Carolinas, and from northern Alabama into Georgia. During the Revolutionary War, most Cherokees allied themselves with the British in return for protection against rapacious frontiersmen, and after the war, they signed a treaty with the United States. They observed it faithfully, despite frequent breaches by the federal government. They became acculturated: they were "exemplary" Indians. In profession and conduct, they were Christians. They were "civilized"—peaceful, industrious, productive, educated and orderly. They had a free press and free schools. One of their leaders, Sequoia, invented an alphabet for the Cherokee language, and in 1827 they fashioned a constitution modelled after that of the United States.

Their acculturation did not, however, protect them from the fate that befell all the Five Civilized Tribes: removal. In 1828, Andrew Jackson,[31] known to Indians as "Sharp Knife," was elected President. A frontiersman and a famous Indian fighter, he had nearly exterminated the Red Stick Creeks who sided with the British in the War of 1812. In 1817 he had led troops into Florida, ostensibly searching the Spanish's no-man's-land for runaway slaves. He was, in fact, pursuing the fugitive Indian bands who had collected there to form the Seminole tribe, and his action precipitated the indecisive First Seminole War. Soon after his election, Jackson put through Congress the Indian Removal Bill,[32] which gave him the power to initiate land exchanges with the Indian nations. Removal became complicated by debates over Indian title and sovereignty, and over the conflict between states' rights and federal power (Berkhofer, p. 159), but ultimately it became the basis for the forceful removal of Indians from their ancestral lands to the Indian Territory, the center of which is what is now the state of Oklahoma.

Some support for federal removal did come from proponents who believed that removal was the only alternative to extinction, but many such supporters did not favor removal in the Cherokee case (Pearce, p. 65) and it is clear that the principal impeti to removal were ethnocentrism and cupidity. As General Francis C. Walker, Commissioner of Indian Affairs in 1871, later explained so tellingly: "When dealing with savage men, as with savage beasts, no question of national honor can arise. Whether to fight, to run away, or to employ a ruse is solely a question of expediency" (Collier, p. 124).

Ruses became expedient in the Cherokee case. When gold was discovered on Cherokee lands in Georgia, the Georgia legislature passed a bill confiscating all Cherokee lands, nullifying all Cherokee laws, and prohibiting Indians from testifying in court against whites. Cherokee lands were to be distributed by lottery. Not only did these measures give carte blanche to a swarm of opportunists, but all of these acts, legislative and personal, directly violated existing treaties between the United States government and the Cherokees.

John Ross, the tribe's most distinguished chief, appealed in vain to President Jackson for justice and protection from the invaders. The President and his Secretary of War, Lewis Cass, said the matter was "not one of right but of remedy," but the remedy did not lie with the federal government. The President did not uphold the federal laws and treaties and restrain the state of Georgia or the squatters because he said the executive of the United States could not interfere with Georgia's rightful prerogatives. The remedy, said Jackson, was for the Indians to remove. The Cherokee declined and resorted to judicial appeal, but the Supreme Court refused to acknowledge its jurisdiction in the case, arguing that the Cherokees were not a foreign nation under the constitution. Later, in response to public pressure, it reversed its position and decided that the state of Georgia had no right to legislate for the Cherokee, and its citizens were trespassing on Cherokee land. President Jackson's reaction to the court's reversal was arrogantly self-serving: "John Marshall has made his decision. Let him enforce it" (Debo, p. 186).

Most Cherokees continued to resist displacement. Their land and the gold they were forbidden to mine were stolen, and so were their livestock, libraries, businesses, plantations and food. More ruses were found expedient. Some Cherokee were harried into signing a treaty that ceded the 7,000,000 acres of tribal lands to the United States for $4,500,000, to be deposited to their credit in the United States Treasury. Four hundred of the 17,000 tribal members approved, yet the U.S. Senate ratified this treaty almost immediately.

Still the main body of Cherokee refused to go. Military action became expedient. General Winfield Scott and 7,000 troops rounded up the Cherokee and moved them to what amounted to military detention camps, where they were held in captivity for months. In the winter the Cherokees, many of them barefoot, walked to Arkansas, describing the journey as their Trail of Tears, during which they were struck by the most "melancholy loss of life." Thousands died. While a hundred Cherokees were dying each day, President Martin Van Buren told Congress in December of 1838: "The measures for Cherokee removal authorized by Congress at its last session have had the happiest effects. The Cherokee have emigrated without any apparent reluctance" (Collier, p. 123). The costs of the forced march were charged to the Cherokee credit established by the fraudulent treaty.

The story was much the same elsewhere. By the end of the 1840s, nearly all Eastern tribes had been removed to the trans-Mississippi West.[33] In the Northeast Country, many tribes had been deceived into ceding their lands and relocating in Indian Territory west of the ninety-fifth meridian. Black Hawk led the Sauk and Fox in resisting deportation, but they were ruthlessly beaten down and expelled. The New York Quakers successfully defended a few of the Oneidas, but many were forced to join the Iroquois, the Shawnee, the Delaware, the Creek, the Choctaw, the Chickasaw, the Seminole, and the Cherokee in the area that became part of Oklahoma, Iowa, Nebraska, Missouri and Arkansas. Beyond them were the buffalo-hunting tribes of the Plains, the Sioux, the Blackfoot, the Cheyenne and others, whom it would be expedient to try to annihilate.

Many Americans, especially in the liberal circles of the North, disagreed with Andrew Jackson. It was not a matter of remedy, but a matter of right. "[They] saw the conflict in terms

of Christian humanitarianism and national honor and union"
(Berkhofer, pp. 161-162). Congress was flooded with mail from
communities, churches and other organizations. An
impassioned letter from Ralph Waldo Emerson to President
Van Buren, quoted earlier, expresses the moral outrage and
joins the issues of national honor and Cherokee survival.

...There exists in a great part of the Northern people a gloomy indifference in
the moral character of the government [regarding Cherokee removal]. On the
broaching of this question, a general expression of despondency, of disbelief
that any good will accrue from a remonstrance on an act of fraud and robbery,
appeared in those men to whom we naturally turn for aid and counsel. Will the
American government steal? Will it lie? Will it kill?—We ask triumphantly.
Our counsellors and old statesmen here say that ten years ago they would have
staked their lives on the affirmation that the proposed Indian measures could
not be executed; that the unanimous country would put them down. And now
the steps of this crime follow each other so fast, at such fatally quick time, that
the millions of virtuous citizens, whose agents the government are, have no
place to interpose, and must shut their eyes until the last howl and wailing of
these tormented villagers and tribes shall afflict the ear of the world.
    ... A man with your experience in affairs must have seen cause to
appreciate the futility of opposition to the moral sentiment. However feeble the
sufferer and however great the oppressor, it is in the nature of things that the
blow should recoil upon the aggressor... (Cabot, p. 702).

The unsatisfied "moral sentiment" was particularly
disturbing in the nation that Jefferson had boasted was
honored by all nations[34] "because we are peaceable and just."
In this period the moral contradictions inherent in the Indian
policy, as well as a more general cultural conflict between
freedom and order, caused acute and widespread fear about
national character and national destiny. Jackson had been
right when he said in his First Annual Message to Congress in
1829: "Our conduct toward these people [Native Americans] is
deeply interesting to our national character." In earlier days,
mused Richard H. Dana, Americans had felt called to lead the
world into "the beauty and freshness of Eden" where
humanity was sinless. Now, he thought, cunning and violence
("our conduct towards these people") had corrupted the garden
(Nagel, p. 48). American character seemed "dirtied by a host of
vices" (Nagel, p. 48) and "a want of virtue" (Nagel, p 126).
Numerous commentators observed that the United States was

beset by anxiety and despair.[35] Emerson had been vindicated: "However feeble the sufferer and however great the oppressor, it is in the nature of things that the blow recoil upon the aggressor."

Chapter 3

At daybreak they saw an island... full of green trees and abounding in springs... and inhabited by a multitude of people who hastened to the shore, astounded and marvelling at the sight of the ships, which they took for animals. These people could hardly wait to see what sort of things the ships were. The Christians were no less eager to know what manner of people they had to do with....

An account of Columbus' first encounter with the New World and its inhabitants by his son Ferdinand. Quoted in Fiedler, *The Vanishing American*, p. 38.

The question of "what manner of people" the Native Americans were was to vex the successors of the discoverers in the New World for generations. Columbus described them as:

Artless and generous... to such a degree as no one would believe but him who had seen it. Of anything they have, if it be asked for, they never say no, but do rather invite the person to accept it, and show as much lovingness as though they would give their hearts.... They are men of subtle wit.... I have not found in those islands any monstrous men, as many expected....[1]

Columbus also affirmed that the astounded "multitude" would "easily be made Christians."[2] Early English explorers and colonists shared this view, which was based on the primitivistic "bon savage" notion. Others believed that because the Indians were backward, they, the "artless" and "generous," would be receptive to trading arrangements that would be profitable to the Euramericans.[3] Indian resistance to conversion and acculturation and commerce, as well as the change in the needs, desires and intentions of the Euramericans, such as the need for land for permanent settlement or for cultivation of a cash crop, caused the newcomers to see the monster "many had expected": subhuman and demonic Cannibals, lecherous, cruel, filthy, supersititious and treacherous.

32

By the nineteenth century, perceptions of "the Indian" were becoming tangled. They were complex, ambiguous and varied, though there was one consistency: all aspects of the definition of Indian aggrandized the white people and debased the red. They justified the destruction of the Indians and exculpated the violence of Captain John Smith, the rabid Captain Mosley of seventeenth-century New England, and Andrew Jackson, the foremost Indian fighter of his time. The violence they did to truth prepared the way, in a mythological sense, for later massacres at Sand Creek, Washita and Wounded Knee.

Precedents for the demonic myths and images of these plays can be found in the most widely read American literature of the seventeenth and eighteenth centuries: captivity narratives, sermons, essays and "menace poetry." The sensational blood-and-gore captivity narratives and "menace poems" were the prototypes for nineteenth-century dime novels and twentieth-century cowboy and Indian movies, in which the Indian is a wild menace. In many allegorical **sermons, the Indian becomes an infernal fiend designed to scare the hell and devil out of the listener.**[4] **Even the Puritan** histories preserved the image. In his official account of the Indian wars, *Narrative of the Troubles with the Indians,* William Hubbard says the Indians are moved by "the instigation of Satan, that either envied at the prosperity of the Church of God here seated, or else fearing lest the power of the Lord Jesus, that had overthrown his Kingdom in other parts of the world, should do the like here."[5]

The first and best-known of the New England Indian captivity narratives is *The Sovereignty and Goodness of God, Together with the Faithfulness of His Promises Displayed; Being a Narrative of the Captivity and Restauration of Mrs. Mary Rowlandson* (1682). In it, Mary Rowlandson describes her captors as instruments of Satan: "they acted as if the Devil had told them that they should have a fall... They came home on a Sabbath day, and the Powaw that kneeled on the Deerskin came home... as black as the Devil."[6] Benjamin Franklin described his meeting with the Ohio Indians at a treaty conference in 1753 in similar terms: "In the evening, hearing a great noise among them, the commissioners walk'd out to see what was the matter. We found that they had made a great bonfire in the middle of the square; they were all drunk, men and women, quarreling and fighting. Their dark-colour'd bodies half-naked, seen only by the gloomy light of the bonfire, running after and beating one another with firebrands, accompanied by horrid yellings, form'd a scene that most resembling our ideas of hell that could well be imagin'd."[7]

More favorable portraits of the Indian were drawn in these years, though they were not the rule. In the South, William Strachey and Alexander Whitaker wrote appreciatively about them, and in New England, Thomas Morton, the English renegade who defied the Plymouth colony's regulations and morality by trading and living with the Indians at his Merrymount settlement,[8] wrote *The New England Canaan or New Canaan*, an account of his experiences in the New World. In it the Indians are both emblems of the childhood of man and "scattered Trojans." A like, though somewhat less positive, account appears in William Smith and Thomas Hutchinson's study of wilderness-life warfare, *Historical Account of the Expedition Against the Ohio Indians.*[10] "The love of liberty is innate in the savage and seems the ruling passion in nature. His desires and wants, being few, are easily gratified, and leave him much time to spare.... Hunting makes him strong, active and bold, raises his courage, and fits him for war, in which he uses the same stratagems and cruelty as against the wild beasts; making no scruple to employ treachery and perfidy to vanquish his enemy" (Slotkin, p. 233).

The first of the plays about Indians appeared late in the eighteenth century. Its Indian mythology contrasts with the predominant satanic images from early American literature, and reflects the growing emphasis during the eighteenth century on the noble savage, a phenomenon noted by Nash, Slotkin, Sheehan and Rogin. *Ponteach or The Savages of America* (1766) by Major Robert Rogers, Commander of **Rogers' Rangers and a famous frontier scout, follows the un-**American, principally European, dramatic and philosophic tradition of portraying the Indian as unrestrained, yet uncorrupted and exemplary, living happily and honorably in harmony with nature. This early play deals with the siege of Detroit by Pontiac, the Ottawa chief, and his allies. The critics justifiably judged it "unreservedly insipid and flat" and "one of the most absurd productions... ever seen" (Keiser, p. 68). The white men are unskillfully characterized as stereotyped sadists who rape and kill and exploit the Indians for sport, and the Indians are as crudely glorified as nature's victimized noblemen.

   Tammany, a Serious Opera by Anne Kemble Hatton, first performed in 1794, fared better with the critics. The opera is no longer extant, but the few songs that have been preserved suggest that the native people were represented here also as the stereotyped monarchs of the forest. *The Indian Princess or La Belle Sauvage,* the first of the so-called Indian Dramas, which is also the first of several by J.N. Barker, was performed in 1808.[11] It, too, was successful, playing in all the theaters in the United States and at one in London. The Indian gets no operatic ennoblement, but the acculturated Pocahontas is exalted. There are "good" Indians and "bad" Indians, but as in Cooper, a realistic mixture of the two in any single character does not exist.[12] During the 1820s and 1830s, there was a virtual rage for Indian dramas. Thirty-five were performed in twenty years, perhaps forty by 1860, of which approximately seventeen have survived.[13] Two of the first, George **Washington Parke Custis'** *The Indian Prophecy* (1827) **and** John Augustus Stone's *Metamora or The Last of the Wampanoags* (1829), seem to have inspired the fad which crystallized into a set of conventions and myths. According to literary tradition, Stone was inspired to write *Metamora*[14] by seeing *The Indian Prophecy,* as well as by a $500 prize, offered by the celebrated American tragedian Edwin Forrest, for "the best tragedy in five acts in which the hero, or principal character, shall be an original of this country."[15] *Metamora* was an unprecedented success, used by Forrest continually throughout his career. It was performed hundreds of times throughout the country and was still being played as late as

1887. A rash of plays like it followed. Fourteen of them are included in this study[16] and are noted in Appendix I.

Despite the multitude of authors, performances, sources and historical materials, the images and myths presented by the Indian dramas are few: the same old story, and the same old dramatis personae, and the same old myths and images. The final curtain descends upon the same high crags or whirling waterfall with the tableau of four Indian figures. The young, desirable, aristocratic "Belle Sauvage" is there, one step behind the man, achieving redemption by marrying a white man or dying loyally with the last of the Wampanoags or Norridgewoks or Skikellemus. In either case, she is a "dusky little divinity":[19] pure, merciful and "ripe." She is self-sufficient, submissive, humble, loyal and protective, both maternal and sexual, mother and lover. Near her is the royal forest king, the dignified last-of-the-line, her father or husband, who stands, having accommodated the whites with his domain and daughter, or lies having died for refusing any "accommodation while he lives."[20] In either case he has lived a noble life, dedicated to wars of liberation (in which he is often in league with the British and French). Although he has raised his "red war arm,"[21] he has been more merciful and less treacherous than the third member of the tableau, the Wild Indian.

All the wild Indians in the tableau are seen either with **scalping knives raised on high, or recounting abominable deeds, such as scalping infants "even as [they] drank from the** fountain of the mother."[22] All are murderers, yet not all are satanic. Sometimes they are presented with begrudging admiration as magnificent warriors as well as crude savages. They are exotic specimens whose cruelty is understandable as a cultural trait rather than an act of unmotivated brutality. In any case, all are "worthy to die" (Stone, p. 25), and are either assassinated by fellow tribesmen, killed by the white hero, or done in by their own hands to escape capture and acculturation. They all fall "without a groan" (Owen, p. 203).

The last figure in the tableau is usually on his knees. He is

the tamed savage who has been "fixed" and "altered."
Sometimes he is "shriveled up within his sapless carcass"
(Owen, p. 161) and delivered into a "vile dependency,"[23] in
which "ugh" and "how" are all that is left of the eloquent
oratory of his majestic wild freedom. Addicted to firewater, he
is a malcontent. He complains. He steals. Sometimes, he is
merely pathetic, having yielded to European imagination and
tradition. In any case, he is reduced to describing himself as
"only an Indian,"[24] and "a red child of the great father"
(Deering, p. 48). He is the diminished figure of the child's chant:
"One *little* two *little*, three *little* Indians."

We have then fixed stereotypes: good Indian, bad Indian,
loving Indian, and adjusted Indian, in fixed relationship to one
another. The bad Indian is socially as well as morally inferior
to the good Indian, and often betrays him to the "Yengeese" or
to other Indians. The female Indian is often conceived of as
maternally provident and amorously passionate. Her
Indianness is confined to deft woodcraft and uninhibited
sexuality. She is daughter or wife to the good Indian. The
adjusted Indian can evolve from any of these upon contact
with the invaders. The representation of all is simplistic and
formulaic.

Indian women have been described in exotic terms since
Columbus noted in his journal that they were "naked, well
built, with very handsome bodies and very good faces, well
formed and very comely" (Washburn, p. 4). Amerigo Vespucci
concurred, finding them "of pleasing person, very well
proportioned [and] no more ashamed of their shameful parts
than we are in displaying nose and mouth."

The Indian maiden in the plays is compassionate as well
as comely, royal and graceful as well as pleasing. Intrepid, she
slips through dark forests on errands of mercy or love, her dark
eyes flashing and her gentle bosom heaving. Often her mission
is to save the whites from the treachery of her own merciless
people. Pocahontas, the "dove," saves Captain John Smith's
life in all the plays bearing her name, and in the Owen and
Custis versions she alerts the entire village of Jamestown to
the planned attack of her hawkish father, Chief Powhatan.

In *Pontiac or the Siege of Detroit*,[25] the "fair Indian maid"
Ultina reveals Pontiac's attack plans to the British Colonel
Gladwin. She is driven to help by her compassion for the
potential victims of the "fierce and wily" Pontiac, and for the
starving Indians who have more need of food than war.
Nahmeokee, the wife of the title character in *Metamora*, travels
through a forest teeming with English enemies to reach her
Narragansett brother and enlist his help for the Wampanoags.
She fails and dies as next-to-the-last of the Wampanoags, after
heroically saving the delicate white heroine from her fellow
tribesmen. Oolaita of *Oolaita, An Indian Heroine,* would
willingly die, like Pocahontas, for unappreciative Christians
whom her Sioux king-father calls "vile reptiles." She does save
a pair of newly-weds and their guide, first from her father and
then from a band of warriors who discover them on Lakota
land. "What!" says she, "Murder beauty, innocence and truth?
What! Kill thus fiend-like a defenseless woman? Away, be
gone, or fear the power of Machwita's daughter!" In Joseph
Doddridge's play *Logan, the Last of the Race of Skikellemus,
Chief of the Cayuga Nation,*[27] a bereaved mother, Queeta,
successfully pleads for the life of a young white captive whom
some of the war chiefs want to roast. She wishes to adopt him to
replace the son she has lost in the massacre at Yellow Creek.

Even the most destructive woman in all the plays,
Melinda-of-the-Morn, follows suit. Also known as Sweet Sky,
this chieftain-daughter of Pontiac is the fellow warrior and
betrothed of Tecumseh in *Tecumseh and the Prophet of the
West, an Original Historical Israel-Indian Tragedy* by George
Jones (1844).[28] This "proud-necked" beauty rescues her Anglo-
image, Jessie McDonald, from the monstrous intentions of The
Prophet, brother to Tecumseh, a favor that is later
reciprocated. Moreover, she guards Tecumseh against the
machinations of his ambitious brother and also those of the
degenerate traitor, Winnemac, declaring boldly that "her heart
is strong and will defend them with the wild devotion of a
woman."[29]

In the Pocahontas plays, the title character is usually
depicted at first as a "princess au naturel": regal, eloquent,

noble but nonetheless, according to the testimony of other characters, a barbarian. However, none of her acts on stage (apart from the killing of an occasional bird) and none of her attitudes (aside from a faintly suggested sexual enthusiasm) confirm these imputations. Her only evident barbarous quality is ignorance, and she is fundamentally genteel. She is converted to Christianity and civilized refinement through her ardent love of Rolfe, Captain Smith's aide, and by her immediate and unexplained veneration for Smith. The marriage with Rolfe is celebrated as an instance of wild nature tamed and an omen of peaceful white-red relations in the "virtuous empire in the west!" (Barker, p. 627).

In *The Indian Princess* by J.N. Barker, Pocahontas rejects her native betrothed, fierce Miami, a Susquehannock who wants to take her to his cabin adorned "with scalps and skins." She favors instead Lieutenant Rolfe, with whom she falls in love at first sight in a "wild and picturesque" (p. 570) grove in this "fairy land of fertility" (p. 589). In this land of "free atmosphere and ample range / The bosom can dilate, the pulses play / And man, erect, can walk a manly round" (p. 580). They embrace and kiss, and Pocahontas asks him to be her lover. They return to her father's lodge at Weocomoco, she "leaning on him with innocent confidence" (pp. 601-611). This is decribed by Pocahontas' attendant, Nima, who has meanwhile been with Robin, a suitably menial Englishman. Putting hand to heart, she says, "Princess, white men are pow-wows. The white man put his lips here, and I felt something here." Pocahontas' love affair with Rolfe proceeds honorably, she renouncing her country's idolatry and accepting "heavenly truths... and sentiments sublime, sweet and social," and he petitioning her father, King Powhatan, for her hand.

The relationship between Robin and Nima and between members of Smith's command and various enemy squaws is less idealized. When Robin first sees Nima, she responds so dramatically that he observes: "A personable fellow shall have his wench anywhere.... Well, my dusky dear, how could you like such a man as I am?" (p. 599). She asks if he is a man, and he responds, "I'll convince you of it some day." Later, after he has "crept into the heart" of the "dusky divinity," he describes himself as one of the "Lords of Creation" (p. 610) and Nima as his "plaything" (p. 627). At the end, he gives an accounting of their relationship to another European, describing Nima as "a wild thing, sir, that I caught in the wood here. But when I have clipped her wings, and tamed her, I hope (without offence to this good company) that we shall bill without biting more than our neighbors" (p. 608). More "wild women" in need of taming, described as "divers colour'd fruit waiting to be plucked" (p. 610),[31] are encountered by the Englishmen in their participation in the war with the Susquehannocks as allies of Powhatan:

> Her squawship's maids of honour were the maskers;
> Their masks were wolves' heads curiously set on,
> And, bating a small difference of hue,
> Their dress e'en such as Madam Eve had on
> Or ere she eat the apple....
>
> They glisten'd most gorgeously unto the moon.
> Thus each a firebrand brandishing aloft,
> Rush'd they all forlorn, with shouts and frantic yell,
> In dance grotesque and diabolical,
> Madder than mad Bacchantes.
>
> A beauteous wolfe-hound came to me....
>
> And let me with her pine torch to bedward,
> Where, as the custom of the court it was,
> The beauteous wolfe-head blew the flambeau out,
> And then....

And then the gallant but innocent American-to-be, Walter, comrade of the apotheosized Smith, reassures his wife, Alice, he went to sleep: these wolfe-heads cannot compare with his "melting, rosy non-pareil" (p. 608).

The Pocahontas of Custis is also royal, dark complexioned, well formed, courteous and discreet (p. 194). Like Barker's character she is a "gentle fawn of Virginia" (p. 198) who rejects her Indian lover despite her father's wishes because he is too fierce and vindictive for a "Christianly merciful" girl who comes near to being a caucasian. Again the white men are "pow-wows" for the Indian maids, and Pocahontas muses "I know not how it is, but my attachments become fixed upon the strangers the first moment I beheld them" (p. 191). She marvels at their "shining arms... air of command... lofty carriage." They seem to her "like beings from a higher world sent here to amaze us with their glory" (p. 194).

Notwithstanding all the piety and gentility, the princess is still "a nimble fawn" in a "wild garden of nature" full to "wantonness of health and spirits" (p. 193). Another Indian maiden of the Pocahontas cycle, Amaya, straightforwardly urges her lover to take off his English dress and resume his "primitive nakedness and liberty" (p. 93).

Robert Dale Owen goes even further in this direction. His Pocahontas is "a rare wench," and she is not Christianized, although she is merciful and honorable. She does not reject an Indian lover for a white, though she does save Smith and marry Rolfe. Smith is obviously disappointed when she does not requite his romantic interest in her: he winces as she says of him "I love to call him my father" (p. 105). This Pocahontas is uniquely independent, "a tameless spirit" who teases the brave "Indian Apollo" Paspaho that he dislikes the "sickly skinned" because he fears they will steal the Indian maiden's heart. Such insubordination by an Indian woman to an Indian man, or any man, is peculiar to this play, despite its appropriateness in a woman who defies her lordly father. This free-thinking Pocahontas also ponders marital equality while talking with her conservative sister Nomony. She would like to be the object not only of desire but also of the soul's affection, "not to crouch behind, but to stand beside."[33] Nomony calls these "Yengeese thoughts" and articulates the role of the Indian wife in these plays: "I am content to prepare a hunter's meal, care for his children, if need be, till his field. Our mother labored thus for our father and she surely knew what was right to do" (p. 149). Nomony acts instinctively and marvels that pre-Rolfe Pocahontas has not yet loved. "It is so natural a thing to love! So difficult to keep one's heart from loving" (p. 68). Nomony embodies the settler's dream of the dark-eyed, submissive, hard-working native woman, "ripened prematurely" (p. 52) and who "go[es] without a petticoat" (p. 36) in the "wild woods" (p. 52). Anne, the eligible English woman, is much harder to get. She keeps her heart from loving even more readily than Pocahontas.

The only Pocahontas play written by a woman is *The Forest Princess* by Charlotte M.S. Barnes, published in 1844 and inspired, according to the author, by Stone's *Metamora.* Again, Pocahontas is an "animated type of mercy and peace, unselfishness and truth... and benevolence" (p. 149). Her life is "pure, active, affectionate" (p. 149), and her death, a unique scene in these Pocahontas plays, is "beautiful, Godly, and Christian" (p. 149). But she is less readily accultured to the white man's ways and means. Still trying to temper her father's wrath with mercy, she shares his anger at white treachery and deceit toward Indians (and toward one another) and like him is furious at the ambition of the Dutchman, Volday, who, Kurtz-like, would like to live "in lawless luxury... and reign amid these forests!" (p. 182). She is loyal to both her father and her husband, promising not to desert her father in his old age and assuring her husband Rolfe that "Whene'er a forest maiden gives her heart / Around her the Great Spirit casts a spell; / Before her eyes the husband of her soul, / Even while absent, ever seems to stand, / And from her sight shuts out all other men" (p. 22). In the Pocahontas-female-savior tradition, she rescues Smith and exposes the treachery of Volday, thereby saving Rolfe and the colony. The final act of this play is set in London. In scenes at court with a sympathetic and helpful Prince Charles and Queen Anne, she and Smith clear Rolfe of false charges of treason. As she dies in Gravesend, on the eve of her intended return to Virginia, Barnes' Pocahontas has a prophetic vision of George Washington, "the Genius of Columbia," standing near Powhatan. She predicts that many noble chiefs shall arise from her beloved soil,

But one o'er all

> By heaven named to set a
> nation free,
> I hear the universal world
> declare
> In shouts whose echo
> centuries prolong,
> The Father of his Country!
> O'er the path
> Of Ages, I behold Time
> leading Peace.
>
> (pp. 263-264)

She refers to the reconciliation of the "Island Mother and Giant Child" (pp. 263-264) by their bonds of love and language.

The heroine's marriage in all the Pocahontas plays symbolizes the union of white and red in love and in the collective enterprise of building "a great and glorious American Empire," and Barnes' Pocahontas has the authority to express and interpret the symbolism, a role heretofore given only to male characters.

Only in *Oolaita or the Indian Heroine* does a woman hold the central and title part. Oolaita, like Pocahontas, is steadfast in her love of a young and merciful suitor, Tallula, despite her king/father's discouragement and the murderous plots of Tallula's rival, the renowned and treacherous Monona. Like Pocahontas, she is loyal to her love "and from her sight shuts out all other men" (Barnes, p. 221), choosing finally to drown herself rather than marry Monona. *Oolaita*, which preceded all the Pocahontas plays except Barker's, strikes one chord over and over: the mercy of woman, the nobility of mercy, the mercy of the Christian God, parental mercy, and Indian mercy. Oolaita, a sort of gnostic, aware of Christian doctrine, who has rejected her people's violent ways and adopted a milder, sweeter and more merciful course, says:

As for me, a poor, unhappy Sioux, I was raised in this savage wild and taught... war, the chase, peril and toil, and danger. But the Great Spirit who loves the Indian as he loves the Whiteman, gave me a feeling heart as he gave you. Little did you suppose to find in this uncultivated wild... a savage form that owned a Christian soul (Deffebach, p. 20).

Like Pocahontas, Oolaita has a powerful will. She twice defies her royal father, once over burning the captives and again over marriage with Monona, "first of chiefs but first of villains" (p. 33). She and Pocahontas both protect the lover from the father. She turns away the warriors who capture and intend to kill the innocent Christians. Her lover claims she has the power to heal, along with the ability to pity and forgive. Even the comic, male-chauvinist Indian hater, Dominic, concedes that "There's something noble in Oolaita," and that she is a "good squaw," and he wishes her "a hundred papooses" (p. 14).

Oolaita claims a Christian soul, describes herself as "hapless and spotless," and declares that "though Oolaita's skin were black as night, her soul is pure and spotless as the snow" (p. 14). She is also sister-squaw to Pocahontas in libidinal power. Her first objection to the match with the Monona has nothing to do with his cruelty or ignobility, but with his aged impotence. She snarls at Machwita: "Ungrateful father! Hardened callous man, thus to betroth me to a wither'd limb. What, wed grey hairs, embrace deformity, declining power, and second childhood" (p. 14).

Melinda of *Tecumseh and the Prophet* is as intrepid as Oolaita, and her soul is as spotless, though not Christian. (George Jones, the playwright, refers to all his Indian characters as "Israel-Indians," and he firmly asserts in the preface that "the aborigines of North America and the ancient Israelites are identical for that belief is founded upon the features of form and physiognomy, as well as of religion, customs, and languages" [p. 1]). Jones' dauntless Deborah is not as humble and self-effacing as Oolaita, either as Indian or as woman.[34] Yet, she is just as merciful and "feminine," shedding "pity drops upon the wounds of the famish'd ta'en in battle" (p. 14), and yearning for Tecumseh, who is on a diplomatic mission to the Cherokees. She dreams about the night when Tecumseh will come to her lodge with the calumet of courtship, which she will ritually extinguish, leaving them in darkness.

And when the stars the only watchers are
Thy voice directing, he to thy rose couch will creep,
Whilst thou, to veil thy pure and blissful love,
Wilt joy to shade the illusion'd Calumet.[35]

The "good squaw" wives of the Indian Noblemen Carabasset and Metamora are, like Barker's Pocahontas and Deffebach's Oolaita, possessed of "heavenly truths;.. and sentiments sublime and sweet and social" (Barker, p. 611). That is, they are merciful, kind, religious and "pure as snow." They are loving, exemplary, self-sacrificing mothers, and devoted, faithful and provident wives. Nahmeckee, beloved wife and queen of the title character in *Metamora*, is hardly distinguishable from the virginal Oceana, the daughter of the English regicide (Stone, p. 411), protected by Metamora because of the kindness of her mother, another good woman stereotype, to his father. (The play is based on the life of King Philip, or Metacoma, whose father was Massasoit, friend to the Pilgrims.) A scene in which Nahmeokee is captured by the colonists and cursed by the crowd as witch, hag and Indian seems a feeble effort by the author to differentiate between the red and white women as well as to achieve ironic effect. The wife of the title king in *Carabasset* never appears upon the stage. We know, however, that she has become Catholic, and the French priest Ralle hopes that she will be instrumental in converting her people to Christianity and civilization. However, Ralle's villanous foster child, Ravillac, murders her and her infant son, thereby discrediting the Great Spirit. He has "frown[ed] upon his children" (Deering, p. 48), and the Indians go dig up the hatchet and make it "drink blood" again.

Several Indian girls, daughters of the "Old Squaw Queeta," join their mother briefly at the end of *Logan* in pleading for the young American captive as son and brother. They suggestively praise his beauty and probable hunting prowess and provide him with moccasins for his walk to their wigwam. They promise him that they will love him and be good to him as one of their family.

Despite all the undaunted Pocahontases and their

consistent bravery, the squaws, like the American snowmaidens, suggest cowardice. General Procter of *Tecumseh*, a despicable coward, is characterized as a "squaw," and in Owen's *Pocahontas*, Namontac, just returned from an English court, marvels that the English warriors obey their King, saying, "Their Sachem's an old coward squaw" (pp. 7-8). The warrior chief, Kuhn, in *Logan* asks of Shahillas, fellow chief who has urged his brothers to make peace: 'Must we become squaws?" (Doddridge, p. 23).

Generally, the Indian women of these plays are Les Belles Sauvages, not haggard squaws or maternal fire tenders, and the authors invest them with characteristics that distend the whiteman's ego. They are beautiful and desirable and available, yet spotless, and most significantly, they are the whiteman's perfervid admirers. They reject their Indian lovers, abandon the ways of their people in favor of Christianity and civilization, defy their fathers, and rescue the irresistible whitemen, "beings from a higher world," from the Indian menace. Ever-faithful to their husbands, white or red, they indulge in none of the European adulterous dallying in the wigwams, "shady groves" or "gloomy forests" of these plays. Unlike the dames left behind, these "forest fauns" are not "made of whimsies and caprice/So variant and so wild, that, ty'd to a God/They'd dally with the devil for a change" (Barker, p. 591). They can endure long, arduous journeys, hunt wild animals with bow and arrow, and swim rapids. They can survive independently in a wild environment and are not dependent upon the male for sustenance and survival. They are strong-souled and willful, defying their people's customs and their fellows' wrath. Yet, for the white males of the plays, they are said to give up their identity, becoming timid and shy and submissive. They do not entertain "Yengeese thoughts" (Owen, p. 149) of independence, equality and romantic aggressiveness. Indeed they are nonpareils,[36] providing everything and demanding nothing.

The women are seldom dramatized as mothers, probably because children were too inherently sympathetic. The infant son of Nahmeokee and Metamora is first seen with his parents in a rare scene of Indian domestic bliss. Twice in the fourth act, he is taken from his mother, who successfully begs for his release. Later, after Fitzarnold, the cad, has released both of them as a part of his machinations to have Oceana, a mad mob pursues them, and one soldier spares the child because "the brat is salable." (In fact, the wife and child of King Philip were sold into slavery in the West Indies.) In the last scene, the colonists kill him.

The male counterpart to the Indian Princess is the Indian nobleman, the aristocrat of the forest, golden-tongued, heroically patriotic and honorable. He is a sort of dignified and dedicated benevolent dictator who rules his subjects wisely and who expects their unwavering loyalty. In *Metamora, Tecumseh or the Battle of the Thames, Pontiac* and *Logan* we see this prince at the dramatic climax of a heroic and tragic effort to save his people and their culture from extermination by the whites.

Yet these "grandest models of mighty men" (Stone, p. 10) are not presented as representatives of Indian character, nor is their greatness unqualified. In *Metamora*, the ostensibly orphaned Walter, who is revealed later to be the son of a nobleman and then marries the delicate heroine, observes to Metamora: "Were all thy nation mild and good like thee, how soon the fire of discord might be squenched" (Stone, p. 12). The beloved Oceana agrees to the Chief's virtues, but objects, "He is a heathen" (p. 12).[37] Tecumseh is described as "rude yet great" (Emmons, p. 35), and the heroic Pontiac "knew no bounds to his warlike ambition" (Macomb, p. 56). Two of the Indian chiefs in *Logan*, Tawatwee of the Shawnees and Kuhn of the Wyandots, are vengeful, warlike and cruel. "I hope for prisoner for the fire," says Kuhn. "It is a long time since our warriors smelt the burning flesh of a whiteman." "Do it so he shall not die too soon," encourages Tawatwee (Doddridge, p. 24). The unstained Tallula, the young but mighty chief in *Oolaita*, is distinctively generous and merciful among the male Indians, but he describes the wounds of battle as worthy of being **"worshipped and cherished and idolized." Even Jones' Tecumseh, an exemplar of his race from the Anglo-European** point of view, is aroused to a frenzied cruelty when General Harrison, with whom he is parlaying in Vincennes about the validity of land treaties, warns him to honor the suspect Treaty of Grenville. He replies:

> Then Chief! like raindrops shall the pale face fall!
> The nuptial song shall cease 'neath midnight yells;
> The Bride, her death on couch of love shall find;
> The youthful wife sha'' bear her unborn, dead!
> And mothers to their hearts shall children fold
> And in their phrenzy shriek with terror wild.
>
> (Jones, p. 34)

Carabasset is "so noble yet, also so erring" (Deering, p. 16).

The principal defects attributed to these noble sachems are the ferocious and vengeful practices of war (scalping, burning at the stake, mutilation, killing of innocent civilians) and an unforgiving, merciless attitude toward their enemies. These heroes, however, are the most merciful of the Indian warriors of these plays.[38] They are more "Christian." Metamora "loves the mild-eyed and the kind" (Stone, p. 11) and criticizes the whites for the heathenish hardness in expelling a nonconformist (presumably Roger Williams) from their colony: "If my rarest enemy had crept unarmed into my wigwam and his heart was sore, I would not have driven him from my fire nor forbidden him to lie down on my mat.... Your great book... tells you to give good gifts to the stranger and deal kindly with him whose heart is sad; the Wampanoag needs no such counselor, for the great spirit has with his own fingers written it upon his heart" (Stone, p. 20).

Metamora also saves the incipient all-American boy, the simple and unaffected Walter the heroine's lover, from burning. Tecumseh is criticized as a "squaw" by his counselor Maycock for weeping at the sight of a baby scalped "even as it drank from the fountain of its mother" (Emmons, p. 14). Later, he keeps Maycock from torturing an American captive. In spite **of his need to avenge his wife's murder, Carabasset mercifully** yields to the supplications by a settler for her small son. He also spares the well-intentioned priest, Ralle, though he is foster father to the murderer of Carabasset's wife. In *Logan*, the title character, chief of the Cayugas, and Shahillas, chief of the Ottaways, dissuade the other chiefs from sanctioning the burning of the American prisoner: "Shahillas is ruthless in war, but merciful in peace!" (Doddridge, p. 19). Logan is criticized as "soft-hearted" (p. 27) for his friendship with whites.[39] Logan and Shahillas also deplore all bloodshed except that necessary for vengeance, a religious duty, and they are ever-mindful of the women and children's safety. In Barker's *Indian Princess*, Pocahontas' mercy and bravery are seconded by her brother, Prince Nantaquas, who protects Smith from the bloodthirsty braves and pleads with Powhatan for the captive's life. Tallula of *Oolaita* is exemplary in his compasion, piety and faith. Early in the play, he appears in a raging thunderstorm and apostrophizes: "Here sleeps a quiet conscience. And, in piece and joy, an upright heart; I have a hand untarnished by man's blood. But sure there's none will harm me—sure there's none will lift the direful instrument of death against a poor, defenseless, harmless youth" Deffebach, p. 32). He prays for strength, justice and self-defense. They are granted forthwith, "for heaven stands faithful by the brave and just" (p. 32). Tallula successfully defends himself against two white assassins, hired by the jealous Monona, killing one of them. The other pleads for mercy: "Savage by name, but I trust not by nature, pity, forgive, and have mercy on a whiteman" (p. 34). Tallula grants him his life with the injunction: "And through your life remember this great truth / The Indians too can pity and forgive" (p. 34). Later, Tallula shortsightedly grants Monona his life also, becoming an unwitting accomplice in Oolaita's suicide. At the end, he whose "arm was never raised / T'inflict an injury or sustain a crime" (p. 42) stabs himself in grief over Oolaita's death, and, as he dies, he forgives her father and Monona.

Jones' Tecumseh is also merciful whether the victims are red or white. He does not "sanction bloody deeds" (p. 51). He deplores his brother's burning of the visiting Delawares; he orders Harrison protected in battle because he tried to avoid

war. He sheds "pity drops" on his mother's grave and on seeing
the Indian corpses. (No other dead are visible on the
battlefield.) In the prologue to his play *Pontiac*, Alexander
Macomb allows that Pontiac and his people are, indeed,
indiscriminately vengeful and cruel, but explains their fury as
a response to white injustices:

> When first we saw him in his pristine state
> The native knew not what it was to hate....
> The stranger then might move through all the land
> And meet the savage with a naked hand;
> A hearty welcome in the wigwam find,
> And every treatment of a generous kind.
> (Macomb, p. 9)

Indian generosity and hospitality are praised in the other
plays. Despite his advisors' counsel that the colonists will seize
all the land and food, Powhatan in Owen's play insists there is
enough for all. In Barker's representation, Nantaquas, brother
to Pocahontas, gives food to the enfeebled English during
Smith's absence. Metamora vows not to use his worst enemy
spitefully if he comes to his wigwam for help. Logan swears
that, until his family was massacred: "I appeal to any white
man to say, if ever he entered Logan's cabin hungry and he
gave him not meat; if ever he came cold and naked, and he
clothed him not... such was my love for the white man."[40] The
gentle and delicate Edith, fragile aristocratic emigrant in *Nick
of the Woods*, who travels from the east coast to the
unidentified wilderness, remarks that "a kinder and more
hospitable people exist not upon the earth."[41] One of the white
hired guns in *Oolaita* confirms Tallula's assertion that whites
who plead for mercy or ask protection at the Sioux cabin are
never denied. After offering the threatened American
messenger a bed in his wigwam, Jones' Tecumseh advises his
braves: "He is within the circle of my home; and though my
enemy and his long knife were reeking with the blood of a
Shawnee, he should be safe! The Indian does not yield to any
race in deeds of hospitality!" (p. 41).

The threat of loss of personal or tribal freedom motivates

much of the heroic Indian action in the plays. Metamora declares, "The Wampanoag will not wrong his white brothers... but he owns no master," (Stone, p. 12) and vows that his son "shall not be the white man's slave" (p. 17). Like Patrick Henry, he urges liberty or death: "Freedom! Our lands! Our nation's freedom! Or the grave!" He stabs his willing wife to prevent her enslavement and defies the whites until they shoot him, crying "We are destroyed—not vanquished" (p. 39).

Pontiac regards his duty to his own people as his greatest duty: "We are poor, but not so depressed as to forget that it is our duty, as well as our interest to protect our race from the oppression of strangers" (Macomb, p. 19). He refuses even in captivity to "yield with life to any accommodation," (p. 48), and as he dies of wounds inflicted by his Brutus-like counselor, he cries, "I die with my country" (p. 55).

In *Logan*, despite arguments that the whites are "like an ant hill; you may tear down a part of it and kill a great many, but there are always enough left to build it up again" Doddridge, p. 17), the chiefs vow to live free or die. Emmons' Tecumseh recognizes that his personal liberty would be compromised by accepting either English gifts or English values. He turns down the epaulettes and military sashes offered by the cowardly General Procter and says, "T'would cramp my limbs in native wildness free" (p. 30). He fights to the death to protect that sense of liberty. Carabasset, too, stoically chooses death to slavery: "Better to perish thus than breathe as slaves" (Deering, p. 33).[42] The proud Powhatan refuses to kneel at Smith's coronation ceremony. Even less accommodating than the Powhatan of Custis' play, Prince Matacoran departs westward with this prophecy: "In a long distant day, when posterity shall ask where rests that brave, who disdaining alliance with the usurpers of his country, nobly dared to be wild and free, the finger of renown will point to the grave of Matacoran" (Custis, p. 208).

The finger of renown, though, was also the finger of accusation. Though selfless dedication to liberty was presented as a part of "that lofty bearing, that majestic mien— the regal impress that sits upon his [the Indian's] brow," the means employed to maintain it become "part of the character of the savage who is distinguished from the civilized Christian... in protection and forbearance in gentleness, and in all those goods" (Boucicault, p. 17). Metamora warns the intruders,"Do not tread too hard upon the serpent's folds. His fangs are ñot taken out, nor has his venom lost the power to kill" (Stone, p. 22), and he prays like an Old Testament warrior for help from Manito:

Break thou the strength of the oppressor's nation, and hurl them down from the high hill of their pride and power, with the loud thunder of thy voice. Confound them, smite them with the lightning of thy eye—while thus I bare my red war arm (p. 37).

Although the point of view in *Logan* is sympathetic toward the Indian and more dramatic attention is given to the heinous intentions of some whites, the two exemplary chiefs, Logan and Shahillas, agree that vengeance is a duty to the victims of the unprovoked attacks, to their fathers, and to the Great Spirit. The red hatchet must be lifted, they conclude, and Shahillas warns the young men that if they turn to run in battle, they will "die by my hands" (Doddridge, p. 20). Emmons' Tecumseh asks for no supernatural intervention, but declaims his own superhuman, martial powers: "Her gallant maw the wolf shall cram with quivering flesh! The cat strip the bones! Aye, tremble shall the mountains at my voice—for they shall fear it as the thunder" (p. 9). But Tecumseh dies, "the last of all my race" (Stone, p. 35), and Manito frowns upon the last of the Wampanoags. "White Gods are greater than Gods of the Indian" (Custis, p. 29) concludes the fierce Prince Matacoran as he exits. "Bold as a lion" (Macomb, p. 51), Pontiac "goes down to the dark valley" (p. 23).

Even the best of Indians was reviled for his religion, sometimes presented as devil-worship, usually as superstition, and always as prompting the deplored vegeances. The noble male savage, unlike the Indian princess, did not know "heavenly truths." "The chief traits of Indian character are gratitude and superstitious revenge" (Owen, p. 223), says

Owen in the afterword to *Pocahontas*. Other playwrights acknowledged the latter in the action and characters of their plays. Deering ascribes Carabasset's reign of terror to dutiful revenge as well as personal hatred. Owen has a warrior try to kill Smith to satisfy the bloodthirsty Hobomoc, a malevolent god who manifests himself as a snake. Tecumseh and Pontiac pray both to the God of Lightning; all the priests and Powhatan interpret natural events as supernatural signs; vengeance is generally assumed to be a divine commandment. In *Logan*, Tawatwee sees owls, northern lights, and the scarcity of pigeons as signs indicating a war of retaliation is at hand. Kuhn describes the constant war in the animal kingdom (including humanity) as "the will of the great spirit" (Doddridge, p. 13), and all agree that "the Spirits of our friends will never rest until we have revenge upon the whites" (p. 17). In *Oolaita*, the Indians are described as "worshippers of brazen images and wooden gods" (Deffebach, p. 11), and the heroine herself decries her father's assertion that "forgiveness, mercy, pity, and compassion are strangers to my bosom" (p. 18): "He who willfully destroys another," she warns, "is awfully hateful to the Great Spirit's eye" (p. 18). Although Tecumseh refers to "Manitou," not Jehovah, most of Jones' "Israel-Indians" are represented as pious Jews. General Harrison compares Tecumseh to Moses as as a deliverer of his people from bondage, for instance. But the "bad Indian," the Prophet, burns the Delawares for their "witchcraft" and believes in his own supernatural, demonic powers.

Thus, the writers credit the typical noble savage with an awesome array of virtues—honor, generosity, hospitality, gallantry, dignity, eloquence, patriotism and fearlessness— and then discredit him for his cruelty, vindictiveness, technological underdevelopment and paganism. The combination renders him a worthy opponent and an estimable trophy for the Anglo-Europeans, "beings from a higher world" who always defeat him and usually kill him, into the last survivor of the race."

These flawed aristocrats, these noble savages, are consistently contrasted with the pitiless and vicious wild

Indian. "I am Wenonga the Black Vulture of the Shawnees; I am Wenonga and have no heart" (Medina, p. 29). Here are the monstrous men Columbus failed to find. The wild Indian whoops, howls hideously, performs the war dance, paints himself, brandishes tomahawk and spear, lusts for revenge and collects human scalps, large and small. He is presented as more representative of his race than the Metamoras or Carabassets or Pocahontases. He is shown throughout as disposed to filth, and given to deviousness, treachery, vengeance and heathen ferocity.[43] He is described in the imagery of wild animals, devils, and "red niggers" (Medina, p. 24).

Metamora's prophet, Kaweshine, yearns to burn the innocent prisoner for his "lips are dry for the captive's blood" (Stone, p. 20). Metamora's enemy urges fellow colonists, " 'Tis time to lift the arm so long supine, and with one blow cut off his heathen race, who spite of reason and the word revealed, continue hardened on their various ways, and make the chosen tremble" (p. 20). An American soldier in *Pontiac* complains, "These tawny rascals are more like serpents than human beings. They hide in the grass and bushes and never fight fair" (Macomb, p. 50). Even Pocahontas acknowledges this quality, albeit as criticism of the deceitful colonists who have imprisoned her despite an agreement with her father, whom they described as "treacherous:"

> Ye blame the red man, yet adopt his wiles.
> Why do ye practice treachery, deceit,
> Trampling on hospitable gratitude
> By thus constraining me? Oh shame.

In the *Octoroon,* the wooden "Inginn," Wahnotee, is "naturally suspected" (Boucicault, p. 10), despite lack of evidence, of having killed his friend, the "yellow boy" Paul. Despite the presence of an Iago-like white man, Ravillac, whose "motiveless malignancy" prompts patricide, infanticide, rape and murder, and despite the bitter, vindictive conflicts between the Catholic French and the Protestant English, it is the Indians only in *Carabasset* who are accused of ferocity.[44] Father Ralle, humble and kind French Jesuit, argues against the alliance of his countrymen with "a wild, revengeful race who will fire at night / The widow's humble cottage" (Deering, p. 13), a race of savages with "fires raging within" (p. 15), who will "plunge again in blood" (p. 16). Awaiting the return of warriors who have been avenging the murder of Chief Carabasset's wife, Father Ralle, whose conversion rate has been meager, wonders: "Who can control the savage in his fury? Then he is like the tiger who hath drunk of human blood—nought else can satisfy and in his burning thirst for vengeance may fasten we know not where" (p. 35). Even the gentle Adelaide, the white heroine who is rescued from Ravillac by Carabasset, comments on the red man's indiscriminate revenge: "The red man's wrath is dreadful; friend and foe are now alike to him" (p. 27). And Telie in *Nick of the Woods*, the sentimental, self-sacrificing, white maiden, member of "an extinct race who never existed," rouses herself from a stupor of love for an English aristocrat to rant about "the merciless fangs of the unhuman fiends... who seek to torture and destroy" (Medina, p. 25). This play is dense to the point of obsession with Indian atrocities. Indians murder the mother, sister and bride of the fabulous Jibbernainosay, act as paid assassins, make two unprovoked attempts on the virtuous Roland's life, and justify the epithets of "human wolves," "infuriate tigers" (p. 29), and "red dogs" (p. 13). Wenongo is described as "nigger-in-law to old Satan" (p. 20), suggesting both the infernal and bestial sub-humanness often assigned to color and difference.

In the Pocahontas plays, Powhatan and his tribe are always contrasted with the merciful and just Pocahontas. Only the degree of their ferocity varies. In Custis' play, Powhatan is willing to sacrifice Indian youths to a bloodthirsty God, although he later refuses to sacrifice Pocahontas to his own authority. Namoutac, just returned from England, speaks of his own "nothingness" and his desire to be away from the restraints of civilized society. The tribe had "laid waste" the previous settlement, and Smith accuses them of cannibalism. In Barker's "operatic melodrama," the colonists refer to the Indians as "red rogues" (p. 582), "black fiends" (p. 589) and "dingy devils" (p. 592), and suspect them of cannibalism. Some expect to "be scalp'd and roasted' (p. 580), or to have their "heads parted from their bodies." The savage savage's anger is terrible, and the English speak of his "ruthless hand" (p. 584). Powhatan talks of beheading Smith and attempts to murder all the whites. Miami disgusts Pocahontas because of his "fierce and vindictive" (p. 585) ways, and she declares that rather than marry him, she would "take up my abode with the panther" (p. 603). He swears eternal enmity to the invader and wishes to "feast on the heart of his rival" (p. 616). It is said by the timid Robin that "the Indians wear men's heads... hanging at the breast, instead of jewels; and at either ear, most commonly a child's by way of ear drop" (p. 598).

None of this is justified by the play's action. Powhatan is most amiable and accommodating and plans treachery against Smith and company only when deceived by Grimosco, the priest. Miami, described as "fierce," seems to kill only birds and bears, and argues against sparing Smith's life only because of his unrequited love for Pocahontas. The warriors don't fight but sing a ditty:

> Now we bid the arrow fly—
> Now we raise the hatchet high
> Where is urged the deadly dart,
> There is pierced a Chieftain's heart.
> Where the war-club swift descends,
> A hero's race of glory ends. (p. 606)

When they mention tearing scalps and bringing home "stake devoted" (p. 606) victims, they are not referring to whites, but to Miami's Susquehannocks. No red hands are "wash[ed] in white blood" (p. 600).

Attitudes are much the same in Owen's play. Krabhuis, a Dutch colonist, later shown as a traitor to his fellow settlers, is so consumed with unexplained hatred for "the dirty, heathen

Indians" (p. 30) that he refuses even to listen to their "gibberish" and discredits their hospitality: "We go visiting the Pow-wowing Indians and find them, mayhaps, in good humor;... we are crammed to bursting by the ... savages... but you must stomach a dinner at every dirty lodge, in the village... by way of making friends with the filthy wretches..." (p. 32). Even the sweet, simple, angelic Pocahontas is not spared. He calls her "a dingy, blackhaired savage" (p. 36).

In the victim-at-the-stake-scene that seems to be required, Pontiac's Indians, male and female alike, are described as "merciless wretches and fiends" (Macomb, p. 37), and "infernal savages" (p. 38) who issue "hideous yells" (p. 38). Elsewhere they are compared by the besieged British and American soldiers to dogs, lions, cats and monkeys, but no monstrosities are committed on-stage, and Pontiac's heroic stature redeems everyone.

Not so in Emmons' *Tecumseh*. Even the title character's nobility cannot dim the wild Indian spectacle called Maycock. He is the sadistic scalper par excellence, and inspiration to Herman Melville's "Indian hater par excellence."[45] He displays his wares to General Proctor, the English general who has hired him during the French and Indian War, and proudly asserts that "These me took from out their mother's arms... from the white skull me tore it while yet the life was in him" (Emmons, p. 12). He gleefully described scalping a bride and groom and tearing a "naked skull" from a baby while it suckled. The Prophet, too, is without a heart. He wants to roast the captive Edward and let him "linger in slow fire" (p. 15). While urging the people to frenzied cruelties, he has visions of ghosts "streaming with hot blood" (p. 15). The characteristics of these two in Emmons' play are applied to all the Indians by the American colonel, R.M. Johnson. He describes their deeds: "Our fathers were massacred—mothers butchered, while singing to their cradles. The ivory bosoms of our virgins were stained with blood, the skulls of sleeping infants hacked.... In such a cause, 'tis sweet to die and saint his name with Washington on high" (p 33). The Kentucky riflemen also seem justified in assuming that "the savages are up, each heart convulses, as a caldron filled with blood. We must with valor cool it on the chilly bosom of the earth" (p. 25).

Although not presented sympathetically, Captain Furioso and an unamed lieutenant in *Logan* justify their plan for an unprovoked attack on the Indians by characterizing them as bestial criminals. "An Indian is not worthy to be called a buffalo. He is a wolf, a bear, that lives upon the destruction of everything around him. He is a beast of prey" (Doddridge, p. 8). "An Indian ought to be killed; he is naturally a murderer, and if not at war, it is only because he is chained down by fear" (p. 9). The proposed killing is referred to as "a piece of sport" (p. 11) and the victims as "game" (p. 11).

In Deffebach's play *Oolaita,* the descriptions of the wild Indians, the "mud-colored looking rascals" (p. 26), are given mostly to an unreliable comic figure, Dominic, the guide: "Do you intend to squat down amongst Indians?" He asks Eumelia and Stephen, the runaway newlyweds, "Do you calculate to pitch your tent among a parcel of cannibals, and subject yourself and Eumelia to become the prey of self-opinionated fools?" (p. 9). He threatens to "stick fork[s] into gizzards and cut their yellow throats" (p. 11), before he hides behind the bride's skirts when their captors appear. The captors, however, partially confirm his assumptions. They threaten Dominic and Stephen with torture and Eumelia with rape. Monona, too, is testimony: he tries to murder his rival; he lies to his friend Cachwita; he refuses to hear Oolaita's pleas; and at the end he is banished with instructions to "cry for mercy and forgiveness" (p. 45).

The villainy of the Prophet in Jones' play is more civilized than savage. His patriotism is clouded by his personal ambition. Like Cain, he deceives his twin brother Tecumseh. He tries to kill the latter's fiancee, betrays Tecumseh's pledge, attacks Harrison's troops, advocates burning the white captive who turns out to be the bold white girl, Jessie McDonald, murders the peaceful emissary from the Delaware tribe, and attempts to deceive his fellow-conspirator, Winnemac.

The myth associated with this sadistic monster, represented as more typical than the noble savage, involves gratuitous and indiscriminate cruelty, betrayal of the leader, and retribution, usually death. Obviously these demonic and bestial subhumans who "murder beauty, innocence, and truth" (Deffebach, p. 30) deserve to die, to be "hacked at in a fury of abhorrence and fear." Such skulking savages had to be eradicated like other agricultural pests. The Anglo-Europeans responsible for their deaths and for the deliverance of their victims are worthy of apotheosis as "Lords of Creation" (Barker, p. 610).

The history of this savage native is analyzed and his fate predicted in the preface to *Pontiac*:

> The savage native of this blessed land
> Will now in character before you stand,
> Revengeful, cruel—not by nature so,
> But 'tis because depressed by us so low.
> When first we saw him in his pristine state,
> The native knew not what it was to hate.
> The stranger then might move through all the land
> And meet the savage with a naked hand;
> A hearty welcome in the wigwam find,
> And every treatment of a generous kind...
> The poisonous liquor made the natives mad...
> When thus enfeebled by this dreadful state,
> The wily white men leave them to their fate.

That fate fell to the "domesticated Indian," the "ugh Indian," who also fulfills Smith's prophecy in Owen's Pocahontas play, that the lessons the Indians will learn from their white neighbors are infidelity, immorality and deceit. Pontiac concurs: "Our lands have been seized, our people poisoned, and their morality tainted. Drunkenness and wretchedness are fruits of this intercourse.... The poisonous liquor, which intoxicates our people and debases them to the lowest state, was long forbidden" (p. 32).

Although the Indians in *Nick of the Woods* are described
as besotted and are said to be vulnerable when in drunken
slumbers (Medina, p. 27), nary a drunken Indian appears on
stage. Likewise, Carabasset complains of the "liquid poisons"
which "madden and consume" (Deering, p. 27), and Metamora
accuses the "whiteskins" of giving firewater to his people, but
still, no drunken Indian appears. Nor does he appear in Jones's
Tecumseh and the Prophet, where the "with'ring firewater" (p.
17) is said to have been introduced by the whites and to have
caused Tecumseh's hero, King Philip, to be betrayed. The
redman had been corrupted by drink: "His wisdom mind
Firewater had degraded, laid him low" (p. 43). In *The Octoroon*
(1859), however, a comedy based on stereotyped subhuman
figures (black, yellow, brown and red), the only Indian is a
compulsive drinker, said to do anything for rum. Wah-No-Tee
is listed in the *Dramatis Personae* as "an Indian Chief of the
Lepan Tribe" and is known primarily by the comments of the
characters with speaking parts. Wah-No-Tee only grunts
"Ugh!" (Boucicault, p. 23), "Firewater!" (p. 24), "Rum!" (p. 14),
"Wah-No-Tee" (p. 26), and utters a few unintelligible speeches
in what is described by others as a "mash-up" of Indian,
French and Mexican. He is a "nuisance, who should go back to
the West" (p. 5), a "thief, an ign'ant Inginn" (p. 19), "a child" (p.
23). Zoe, the octoroon, who despises herself and whose only
worthiness is that "our race... knows how to suffer" (p. 23)
denies these accusations: "Wah-No-Tee is a gentle, honest
creature and remains here only because he loves that boy Paul
with all the tenderness of a woman" (p. 5). Eventually the plot
reluctantly and qualifiedly confirms Zoe's appraisal, but not
before Wah-No-Tee is seen trying to steal a gun and taking a
camera while emitting "savage growls" (p. 18), hiding bottles
of rum under his blanket, and stabbing the villain of the piece
"repeatedly" (p. 18). As Berkhofer observes, this Indian figure
was not converted but perverted (p. 32).

One of the other fruits of the intercourse between whites
and Indians was the latter's demeaned self-image, evident in
the tamed Indian of these plays—a castrated male counterpart
to Pocahontas. The proud King Powhatan of Custis'

Pocahontas play is brought low by his self-righteous, Christianized daughter when he tries to administer Indian justice to Smith and the "pallid adventurers" (p. 199).

Cruel King, the ties of blood which bound me to thee are disserved, as have long been those of thy sanguinary religion; for know that I have adjur'd thy senseless Gods, and now worship the Supreme Being, the true Manitou, and the Father of the Universe; 'tis his divine spirit that breathes in my soul, and prompts Pocahontas to a deed which future ages will admire (p. 207).

Powhatan sees the error of his ways and "makes friends" with England because "experience makes even an Indian wise" (p. 208). Even Oolaita, the proud, wilful heroine, debases and discolors herself as a "poor miserable Sioux," one with "a savage form... skin as black as night." She apologizes to those she rescues for her Indian heritage and appearance. In the Pocahontas plays Powhatan bitterly learns adjustment and accommodation to the Jamestown settlers. In *The Forest Princess,* by Barnes, he accepts his race's fate and submits:

Like swollen streams they [the whites] gain upon the land,
And one day will possess it; yes, I hear
My father's prophesying spirit speak
In the low moaning of the forest trees:
He bids me end a useless struggle now,
That red man's portion is decay (p. 209).

And he makes Rolfe pledge to protect Pocahontas when "her kindred are driven from the earth" (p. 233). Similarly, in *Logan,* which is more of a stage debate than a drama, the wise and humane chief, Shahillas, cautions against warring with the white soldiers who have murdered innocent Indians, and he fatalistically urges peace and accommodation:

Whites are many in number, we are but few. They are **rich, we are poor. They** know everything, and we but little. When things begin to run their course, they will go on until they reach their end. Brothers, can we stop the wind from blowing?... If the great spirit says it shall be so, we cannot help it.... The whites will destroy us. We have had our day, our night is at hand. (Doddridge, p. 23)

The implicit self-hatred and the sense of divine desertion

may be seen as the cause of the myriad Indian betrayals. In *Metamora*, the prophet Kaweshine betrays the chief and violates Indian custom because he feels that Manito has deserted his red children. He advises: "Hold out to the palefaces the pipe of peace" (Stone, p. 36). Metamora declines and threatens Kaweshine, who predicts the Wampanoags' divinely sanctioned fate: "Metamora drives me from the wigwam before the lightning descends to set it on fire" (p. 36). Augushaway similarly betrays Pontiac because the latter was ambitious, although his ambition was only to make the British quit the country and "leave us the undisturbed possession of our native empire" (Macomb, p. 48).

George Jones, in the preface to *Tecumseh and The Prophet*, criticizes Thomas Campbell, a contemporary writer, for depicting an Indian chief as "a man without a tear," and says that he intends to do justice to the Indian character. Yet he includes the customary stereotyped traitor. The unconvincing Winnemac yields to "intemperance" and becomes dupe and instrument for the whites. He has "slept in white wigwams" (p. 20). He plots against the Prophet without clear motivation, and against Melinda, who suspects his treachery. He also fails to inform Tecumseh of his brother's machinations, thereby contributing to the catastrophe. For vague reasons, he kills Melinda. Throughout, he is shown alone—spying, eavesdropping, peeping, talking to himself, and at the end, he slinks off, his fate as vague as his character. Carabasset sees his people being seduced by "paltry sums and a few gew-gaws, wrought to deck our persons" (Deering, p. 22), and says they have become "unworthy of the name we bear, submitting to a vile dependency" (p. 23), thus endorsing Father Ralle's image of "poor children of the forest" (p. 5).

In *Logan*, we find not betrayal, but a remarkable amity and unity among the Indian chiefs—a foil to the babel of the whites. Shahillas and the others believe that God has frowned upon them and decreed their defeat: "We have done our duty, but we are too weak for the whiteman. His arm is strong and we cannot hold it" (Doddridge, p. 22).

Pontiac and Smith's common paradoxical prophecy that

drunkenness, wretchedness, debasement and immorality would fell the "savage" when he came in contact with the "civilized" is fully realized in these dramas. The white man's liquor dissolves red character; his commercialism corrupts tribal loyalty; his triumph demeans the red man's proud self-respect and reduces him to penury, humiliating accommodation, or death, all of which the Indian acknowledges: "The red man's portion is decay" (Barnes, p. 209). Then the Indian either joins the enemy, betraying himself and his people, or resigns himself to extinction.

Chapter 4

The white race received a divine command to subdue and replenish the earth.... The black and red races have often felt its ameliorating influences.

Senator Thomas Hart Benton, 1846

To guild our guilt, we've but to call it glory.

John Brougham, *Pocahontas or the Gentle Savage*

"Indians," said Washington Irving, "are like the shepherd of pastoral romance, a mere personification of mere attributes,"[1] a description that obtains in the Indian dramas. None of the figures described in the last chapter are realized as human beings. None is natural or complete; none develops or changes convincingly.[2] Their psychology is simple, their passions restricted, and their lives are centered in action. Most are amoral and lack the capacity for introspection. Some are clearly historical statuary. This demeaning characterization is **furthered by the plots, themes, imagery, forms and settings of these dramas.**

These stage Indians often do not speak of themselves as individuals, but in third-person cliches: "The red man honors a brave enemy" (Barnes, p. 212); "A Wampanoag cannot lie" (Stone, p. 28); "Red men do respect their father's words" (Jones, p. 30); "When the Redskin says, / I am thy friend; and smokes the pipe of peace, / The sun himself is not more sure to rise / From out the forest the morning dawn; / Than he to bide his word" (p. 69).

The language of all the characters is either caricaturing or apostheosizing, both of which dehumanize the character and stylize him out of all particularity and force. Wah-No-Tee of *The Octoroon* is unintelligible: "Ugh!" (Boucicault, p. 41).

64

"Rum! Ugh!" (p. 24). "No, carabine tue": "Paul wunce-Paul Pangeuk" (p. 38). Tecumseh's grammar is childish: "Me hate that stripling warrior" (Emmons, p. 9). The language of all the minor Indian figures is uniformly so simple as to appear moronic. They speak in short, often exclamatory, sentences. They refer to themselves by their given names; their syntax is awkward; their grammar is bad; their words end in "—um."

The language of major characters is turgid and bombastic. As Carbasset is about to leap off a picturesque cliff with the traditional Indian contempt of death, he hesitates long enough to strike a heroic pose and address the English soldiers below: **"Behold / The last of all the Norridgewok hath liv'd / And thus** can die" (Deering, p. 54). Metamora also dies dramatically, issuing garrulous curses:

May the Great Spirit curse you when he speaks in his war voice from the clouds! Murderers! The last of the Wampanoags' curse be on you! May your graves and the graves of your children be in the path the red man shall trace! And may the wolf and the panther howl o'er your fleshless bones, fit banquet for the destroyers. Spirit of the grave, I come! But the curse of Metamora stays with the white man! I die! My wife! My queen! My Nahmeokee! (Stone, p. 40).

There is none of what Thoreau described as "the bow and **arrow twang"** of Indian speech.[3]

The plots of these plays also subscribe to the conventional myths or stories about the American Indian. In all, the male Indian is depicted as submitting to the white soldiers or settlers or dying because he defies them. He cannot win. In the Pocahontas plays, the plot of which "is in every heart" (Owen, p. 21), the heroine leaves the legions of darkness and joins the forces of light by defying her father and marrying Rolfe. The marriage apparently "unites / in peace and love the old world **and the new,"** but actually it is an act of submission; not a union of equals, but of white master and first red servant, or white father and red child. Despite some ceremonial speeches about peaceful co-existence, most plays suggest all Indians will be "driven from the earth" (p. 223), and their fate is "to pass from earth away" (p. 174).

The concluding visions of both reds and whites in the

Pocahontas plays suggest that "the white race... [will] subdue and replenish the earth." Owen's Smith envisions the Indian culture supplanted by "arts and faith of polished, civilized life" and needing "but the hand of industry" (p. 55). This civilized and enlightened labor, he predicts, will be awesomely productive: "They will... hew a road to Glory's farthest goal / And write on her imperishable page / The op'ning chapter of a nation's story" (p. 55). His vision is that "Cities may rise, shall rival Europe's marts / And states sprint up, shall, one day, bear away / The palm of greatness from the Eastern world" (p. 153). The Smith of Barker concurs: "The fine portion of the globe shall teem with civilized society; when arts / And industry, and elegance shall reign, / As the shrill war-cry of the savage man / Yields to the jocund shepherd's roundelay" (p. 627). The colonists' future looks glorious: "A great, yet virtuous, empire in the west!" (p. 627). In Custis' play, Pocahontas looks "thro a long vista of futurity" to a time when "these wild regions shall become the ancient and honour'd part of a great and glorious American Empire" (p. 208).

If co-existence is prophesied, the Indian must become accultured to English Protestant values. He must learn to work harder, believe in Christ, covet property, compete capitalistically, repress or exploit the natural, build cities, and give up the nomadic, martial life the whites mistakenly attributed to them all. Apart from Smith in Barker's play, who thinks "Wild Nature smooths apace her savage frown, / Moulding her features to a social smile," (p. 627) no character is consistently optimistic about the Indians' making such adaptations and becoming de-Indianized. The future of the Indian and his part in the "great and glorious American Empire" (Custis, p. 208) is vague. Powhatan of Custis' play modestly hopes that the story of Pocahontas will become a national legend, and in Mrs. Barnes's play, he hopes only for remembrance: "The red man's name / Will live but in mem'ry of the past" (p. 174).

The Indian's place in American history is more clearly defined in other plays. At first he succors the settlers: "The red man took you in as a little child and opened the door of his wigwam" (Stone, p. 22), providing "a hearty welcome / And every treatment of a generous kind" (Macomb, p. 9). Afterwards the male Indians refuse to accommodate the settlers' ambition and avarice. "Never will Metamora forsake the home of his fathers and let the plough of the strangers disturb the bones of the hushed" (Stone, p. 21). He will not give up land or identity to live as the whiteman's slave. The alternative is death, and the "noble sachems of a valiant race" (Stone, p. 10) are also the last of the race: Shawnees, Norridgewoks, Ottawas, and Wampanoags. "He stakes his life his country to defend / And in that noble duty finds his end" (Macomb, p. 17).

Every play, then, has its "Victory and Virginia" (Custis, p. 191). In many, the Indians are armed only with a just cause. They are defended for resisting white expansion by reference to, but no dramatization of, white injustices such as the invasion and occupation of their lands, the distribution of liquor among their people, the violation of their treaties, the slaughter of their game, the premeditated introduction of diseases, the corruption of their morals, and the murder of their women and children because "nits will be lice" (Doddridge, p. 9). In all these plays, the Indians are the aggressors. It is they who enjoin the battle to the accompaniment of war dancing and war whoops and threats of imminent burnings or scalpings of sympathetic white victims. And always they are defeated.

The white man's inexorable power is attributed principally to two sources, one secular and one divine. In the Pocahontas plays, Powhatan and his tribesmen are awed by the "magical" guns of Smith's party and by the number of settlers. In most of the plays, however, the white men claim that God is on their side and he has given them a divine command "to subdue and replenish the earth."[5] He has given the white man superior weapons and numbers. The white man must, therefore, enact his glorifying role in this divinely-sanctioned history, whether that role is to kill or to be killed. In *Pontiac*, Colonel Gladwin haughtily lectures the lovelorn informer Ultima on God's racial favoritism: "Do you suppose that aught you do or think is not known to me? The Great Spirit watches over his white children and sends guardian angels to advise them of the evil intentions of their enemies" (Macomb, p. 19). The playwright later corroborates the Colonel's credibility. An American negotiator, MacDougal, comes to Pontiac's camp, is taken captive, escapes the fire torture, and is saved from recapture by a French-Canadian lady named Angelique after he has prayed to the Great Spirit for a "protecting angel" (p. 37) to defend him from the fiends. The ultimate victory of the English is credited to divine intervention: "Providence sends our long looked-for vessel to our relief" (p. 46).

Nature and Providence join in justifying the white man in *Logan*. "What ground can an Indian have?" asks a lieutenant responding to the assertion that the proposed Indian victims are "on their ground" (Doddridge, p. 7). He continues:

I would as soon apply to a buffalo for a right to the land....I could prove that he marked the earth with his feet, had eaten the weeds and brushed the bushes with his tail, made the paths to the salt licks, and what has an Indian done more? (p. 7)

The popular philosophy of agrarian idealism proposed that natural law made land ownership dependent upon cultivating or in some way changing the ground by more than leaving an imprint—usually by occupation and labor. Defending the proposed extermination of Indians, the soldier above refutes the charge that the Indians rightfully possess the land because Providence "put the Indians here long before the whites came" (p. 7). "If they had been worthy of its possession, they would have continued in it; but they are Canaanites, whom Providence has doomed to utter destruction."[6] The Captain declares that he is "Joshua come to execute the decree of their destruction" (p. 7).

Identifying the Indians as Canaanites and objects of divine wrath is not enough. They are continually associated with the devil, hell and fiends—"red devils," "infernal savages," "nigger-in-law of old Satan." In Emmons' *Tecumseh* and *Metamora* and Owens' *Pocahontas,* the Indian God is transformed into a merciless enemy, the warfare into a crusade, and the atrocities into strategy.

The red man's gods are not only demonic, but weak and ineffectual compared with the Christian god. The proud Matacoran testifies to the power of the white god and white guns: "The fortune of war is on thy side: thy Gods are much **greater than his [the red man's]"** (Owen, p. 109). **Carabasset** acknowledges that his people have lost divine favor: "Yes, the Great Spirit frowns upon his children" (Deering, p. 48). Kaweshine advises the heedless Metamora: "Manito loves no more the Wampanoag and our foes prevail" (Stone, p. 36). Walter, the Wampanoag's captive, also predicts divine intervention and vengeance "by him who moves the stars and lights the sun" if his blood is shed. Chief Shahillas in *Logan* fears that Indian extinction is divinely decreed: "So says the Great Spirit, His arm is strong and we cannot hold it" (Doddridge, p. 2). Tecumseh vows to fight until thunder, symbol of his war god, smites his breast and his breast is promptly smitten. The dying prayers of both Metamora and Tecumseh for a curse upon the whites go unanswered, and Hobomoc's prophecy that the Longknives will put out their tribal fires with blood is fulfilled. In *Metamora*, Errington threatens the chief with "the wrath of Him who hates the heathen and the man of blood" (Stone, p. 411).

Belief in the holiness of America's manifest destiny—the continued territorial and cultural expansion over the continent—and the correlation of things national and supernatural is at the core of Emmons' *Tecumseh*. Colonel Johnson, inspiring his soldiers before the battle with the Indians, says: "In such a cause 'tis sweet to die / And saint his name with Washington on high"[8] (p. 33). In the final scene, he revives as his soldiers wave the flag over him, and, as the curtain descends, "the band strikes up 'Hail Columbia,' and the Goddess of Liberty descends from the clouds in a car, **enveloped in the Revolving Star of Columbia, accompanied by** Freedom's anthem, bearing in her hand the Star Spangled Banner, the glorious mantle of her Nation's glory" (p. 36). The plays testify in thought and action and theme to the powers of the Anglo's deities. They proclaim Jehovah's divine sanction of American history and his curse upon the heathen red men.

During the 1820s and 1830s, when most of the Indian dramas were written, there was an acute awareness of the plight of the ill-fated Indian As Andrew Jackson allowed, "Humanity... wept over the fate of the aborigines." The weeping, however, was hypocritical. The use of force, deception, threats and bribery by government officials to secure treaties in which Indians ceded their tribal lands was commonplace. As in the Cherokee case, these treaties had been made mere mockery by white encroachment onto the lands guaranteed to the Indians.[9] Other eastern tribes that remained around the edges of white settlements were characterized by demoralization, drunkenness and disease, and many had dwindled to precarious numbers; others were already extinct. Sincere efforts to assimilate the Indians, motivated by humanitarian, commercial and political concerns, had been successful in a few cases, the Cherokee in particular, but, as Ronald Satz observes, "Civilizing the Indians for assimilation into American society never took precedence over pushing them outside the area of white settlement; it merely justified it" (Satz, p. 2). After the "civilized" Cherokee proclaimed themselves a nation with sovereignty over tribal lands, the Jacksonian removal program[10] was put into effect, and they were pushed into the Indian territory.

These facts did "excite melancholy reflections" and widespread public outrage as well. Emerson lectured President Van Buren about "the dereliction of all faith and virtue [and] the denial of justice" in the Cherokee removal case. Sympathetic religionists, trying to bring the Indian within the humane treatment of Western tradition, revived the idea that they were descended from the Lost Ten Tribes of the Jews. George Catlin, the famous painter who traveled among the Indians during the 1830s, recorded his sympathetic encounters with those to be downtrodden by "the grand and irresistible march of civilization":

I have seen him shrinking from civilized approach, which came with all its vices, like the dead of night, upon him... seen him gaze and then retreat like the frightened deer.... I have seen him shrinking from the soil and haunts of his boyhood, bursting the strongest ties which bound him to the earth and its pleasures. I have seen him set fire to his wigwam and smooth over the graves of his fathers... clap his hands in silence over his mouth, and take the last look over his fair hunting ground, and turn his face in sadness to the setting sun. All this I have seen performed in nature's silent dignity... and I have seen as often the approach of the bustling, busy, talking, whistling, hopping, elated and exulting white man, with the first dip of the ploughshare, making sacrilegious trespass on the bones of the valiant dead.... I have seen... the grand and irresistible march of civilization. I have seen this splendid juggernaut rolling on and beheld its sweeping desolation, and held converse with the happy thousands, living as yet beyond its influence, who have not been crushed, nor yet have dreamed of its approach...."

The Indian dramas legitimized "the grand and irresistible march" and made it intelligible by explaining red-white history as an expression of God's will, a "sovereign and irrevocable necessity to all earthly power" (Nagel, p. 67), which was to culminate in "a great, yet virtuous, empire in the West" (Barker, p. 627). Americans, like Joshua, were fulfilling their duty to God and country by enacting His decree for destruction.

The pitiable condition of "the vanishing American" and the vindicating theme of "the grand and irresistible march of civilization" also affected the form in which plays were cast.[12] The subtitles describe one as a "tragedy," another as "An Indian Tragedy," another as "An Operatic Melodrama," and four as "National or Historical Drama." In fact, they are mixtures of melodrama and tragedy in different proportions, all handled with different degrees of confusion. All emphasize the sensational, the picturesque, and the spectacular. The settings are dark and gloomy forests where panthers and wolves and adders live among precipices, high crags and waterfalls. The Vanishing American proudly stalks from his wigwam and is silhouetted against the sunset or declaims metaphorically on the falling autumn leaves. In *Nick of the Woods*, the avenger comes down a cataract in a canoe of fire. At the end of the *Octoroon*, a steamship is set ablaze and explodes. In *Pontiac*, several scenes are spectacles without dialogue which do not advance the action of the plot or otherwise contribute to the story. One features a battle between Indians and combined British and American troops, accompanied by the "most hideous yells and noise" (Macomb, p. 38). The second shows the British being rescued from imminent defeat by the colorful Kentuckians. The third has Pontiac's funeral, which concludes with the sealing of the grave with a stone and the singing of an Indian death song.

In keeping with the melodramatic conventions of the time, the audience gets many thrills: there is much whooping, many alarms, shots, war dances, death songs, painted bodies, threats of torture (unconsummated), charges, duels, romantic subplots and returns of long-lost sons. The costumes and properties frequently include skin dresses, feathered headdresses, war bonnets, furs, tomahawks, peace pipes, scalping knives and war clubs. The audience was to be titillated and gratified by all this picturesqueness, but the strange customs selected were always threatening. There are no dignified and vivid depictions of the Indian's sense of identification and interdependence with all life, none of the Indian martial practice of "counting coup" (touching a live enemy and escaping unharmed), which was more honored than killing the enemy.

The audience's sentiments are excited in other ways as well. In Emmons' *Tecumseh* and in *Nick of the Woods*, there is much gratuitous and gory description of the scalping of infants and mothers, brides and grooms, and ivory-bosomed virgins. "Black-hearted" villains, red or white, plot treacherous machinations, attempt murders, betray their friends and leaders, and suggest abduction or rape. Several plays provide two such villains, one red and one white.

In the Pocahontas plays, this duality has some justification from Smith's account of the episode in his *Generall Historie of Virginia*, but it is treated (there as well as in the other plays) as if to achieve a balance of evil between decadent Europeans and ignoble savages. In Owen's play, Ratcliffe, president of the Colonial Council of Virginia, contrives with his followers to have Smith, a threat to their power and a challenger to their plan to abandon the colony, killed by the Indians. They dishonor their word and imprison

Pocahontas. Smith berates them as greedy and self-righteous hypocrites: "They covet the rich reward a villain earns, / And depreciate the villainy that earns it; / Men who would be at once both black and white; / Would pluck the fruits of Hell on the road to Heaven" (p. 184). Powhatan's counselor, Utta matches Ratcliffe's villainy in degree, if not in kind. He conspires with Powah, an Indian priest, to misinform Powhatan, thereby convincing the chief to murder the white man.

Mrs. Barnes casts Ratcliffe and his underlings, Volday and Francis, as the disloyal conspirators who plan either to attack the savages—"the lawless spirits here"—without provocation or to set sail secretly to England, deserting the sick and helpless. Powhatan, in conjunction with Volday, tries to deceive the white men and intends to kill both Rolfe and Smith. However, his comparison of their respective villainies is thematic: "The red man wars with stranger, enemies; / But thou wouldst slay thy brothers" (p. 205). Maycock of *Tecumseh* is a fiendish rogue, but the bounty for the scalps he takes is paid for by the British General Proctor. Carabasset is said to have taken bloody and indiscriminate revenge for the murder of his wife, but the Frenchman Ravillac is a "pale, sordid knave" (Deering, p. 22), and the English Protestants attack the entire Indian population, not only to avenge their losses, but to "pluck up this root or heresy"—an Indian village with a devoted Catholic priest. Metamora is betrayed by two Indians of "mixed blood," one of whom is said to be willing to accept bribes, but the English colonist Mordaunt is a regicide who is willing to sacrifice his daughter to the profligate Fitzarnold in order to clear his name. English nobility is again evil and decadent in *Nick of the Woods*. The despicable nobleman Braxley has not only stolen the inheritance of the frail Edith and her beloved cousin Roland, he is a "destroyer of virgin purity and peace." Wenonga of the Shawnees, with a "heart of stone," is no worse in intent, although more successful in fact.

The hero of the Pocahontas tragic-melodramas is singular, and pure white.[13] Captain Smith is the conventional melodramatic model of magnanimous virtue. In Barker's play, the valiant and powerful Smith is "always stirring" (p. 582) to make the red men "wise and happy" (p. 587). His means are military, as in Custis' play, but these are considered appropriate here, as with the Turks and Tartars he has already "tamed." Rolfe of Mrs. Barnes' play testifies to Smith's valor, integrity, prudence, generosity, endurance and "pride of conscious worth" (p. 163). Owen credits Smith with spurning the lust for riches that inspires many of his party, and with despising their dishonorable means. Smith apparently loves Pocahontas, but selflessly defers to Rolfe, assuring him that love is the mightiest power on earth and their happiness will be his happiness.

Elsewhere, the heroes are Indians, but they are not "the very model" nor "the first of men." Although they have the tragic hero's greatness of soul, unyielding noble purpose and uncompromising spirit, they are not melodramatically perfect, except in the sense of providing a spectacle. The qualification is in keeping with Aristotle's theories of the flawed tragic hero and the purgation of pity and fear. The flaw, of course, is savagery, i.e., vengefulness, cruelty and paganism, which is treated as a vice in the case of minor figures like Maycock of Emmons' *Teumseh*, but as an unavoidable error in the case of heroes such as Carabasset. It is presented from the point of view of cultural relativism: "They know not what to do." The moral point of view, however, is absolute—they are wrong. In other words, they incur guilt guiltlessly.

The Indian heroes' flaws cause their downfall. Yet often, as Pearce points out, their savagery seems contrived and imputed. Metamora is an honorable and sustaining friend of the colonists, a protector of female virtue, and a sentimental father. He does make war, but he is forced to by the white greed and injustice. In Custis' *Pocahontas*, the principles of the **"rude" Matacoran are indistinguishable from those of the hero** Smith. Pontiac is said to take pleasure in war; he seizes a pseudo-peacemaker; his assassin accuses him of knowing "no bounds to his warlike ambition." Yet the warlike ambition is to repel the invaders and protect his homeland, and he is reluctant to torture the captives. Emmons' *Tecumseh* is ferocious in expressing his patriotism, and Jones' Tecumseh rants, but they act rationally, mercifully, and even with refinement, except that their English is problematic.

There are few American villains. Aside from Church in *Metamora*, villainy is attributed primarily to the savage savages and to the decadent Europeans, noble and common alike. The pre- and post-revolutionary patriots, as noble as General Harrison of Jones' *Tecumseh* or as common as the Kentucky rifleman of Emmons' *Tecumseh,* are honorable men. Often, they are young: Walter of *Metamora*, the newly-weds of *Oolaita,* the young lovers of Jones' *Tecumseh* and Stone's *Metamora,* and Robin of Barker's *Indian Princess.* More often, they are competent woodsmen and Indian fighters who compete with and best the British. They are simple and unpretentious, which sometimes makes them comic figures, like the heroic but lawless Captain Ralph Stackpole of Medina's play, who speaks in Mark Twain-like hyperbole and malapropism, but who saves the settlers and the ridiculously refined and impotent English refugees who have mysteriously arrived in the American wilderness. Most often, they are moralistic patriots who believe in God and country and are innocent of the immoral egocentricity and the equally immoral lack of restraint that the Europeans and the Indians respectively represent. They stand ennobled between the decadent and the primitive.

The endings of the plays, along with the characterization of the flawed but exceptional hero who passes from happiness to misery, are more tragic than melodramatic. The audience's pity is often purged by concluding visions and prophecies of American greatness divinely ordained. The Manifest Destiny conclusion appears in all the Pocahontas plays. In Barnes' version, Captain Smith describes his Aeneas-like mission in Virginia, "to hew a road to glory's farthest goal / And unite upon her imperishable page / The opening Chapter of a nation's story" (p. 23). The humbled Powhatan of Owen's play hopes for little—"May we hope that when the tales of early days are told from the nursery, the library, or the stage, that kindly will be received the national story of 'Pocahontas or The

Settlement of Virginia' " (Owen, p. 60). The prologue to *Pontiac*
refers to this "blessed land" (Macomb, Prologue), and to the
forms Providence takes to ensure the defeat of the Indians,
forms such as the American troops, who save the day nearly
lost by the inept redcoats. As Emmons' Tecumseh dies, the
Goddess of Liberty descends from the clouds. In *Metamora* the
Chief of the Council concludes: "Surely a land so fair was ne'er
designed to feed the heartless infidel" (Stone, p. 406). Later, he
warns Philip to fear "the wrath of him who hates the heathen
and the man of blood" (p. 412), and his subordinate observes:
"Heaven smiles on us—Philip is in our power."[14] **The action**
confirms the colonists' beliefs. Although Jones' Tecumseh
believes that Indians and whites have the same God, he
expects divine favor on the grounds of justice rather than race.
He is disappointed, and, as he dies, concedes that white
legendry is part of God's plan.

In *The Octoroon*, Nature lends justification to the white
man's dominance: "Nature has said that where the white man
sets his foot the red man and the black man shall up sticks and
stan' around" (Boucicault, p. 18). This natural superiority
requires "protection and forebearance, gentleness, and all
them goods that show the critters the difference between the
Christian and the Savage" (p. 18), qualities found in "a real
American heart, busting up with freedom, truth, and right" (p.
18).

Thus, the suffering and death are made meaningful, and
pity for the noble savage's fate and fear of the wild Indian's
ferocity are theoretically purged. Natural as well as divine law
provides that these inferior people, however noble in their
savagery, must be sacrificed to the consecrated American
destiny of the "Virtuous Empire" and must be removed by
those who have been charged with what Daniel Webster called
"The Sacred Trust." This anticipates Longfellow's
"Hiawatha," who, before he sails into the "glory of the sunset,"
advises his people:

> Listen to their words of wisdom
> Listen to the truth they tell you,

For the Master of Life has sent them
From the land of light and morning.[15]

It is apparent that "National Drama" in this context meant an exonerating literature compounded of melodrama and tragedy: operatic scenes; heartless villains; triumphant, pure white heroes; tragic Indian heroes; tragic plot progression; tragic purgations. Most significantly, Manifest Destiny becomes the legitimizing force that is as inexorable, merciless and inscrutable as the fate of Oedipus.

Zealous patriotism paved the way for this juggernaut of Manifest Destiny. Owen's Smith, a patriot who preceded his country, challenges his subordinate's argument that they should abandon the settlement in the New World because no gold or pearl fisheries or routes to the South Seas have been found. He praises the country's beauty and its political and commercial possibilities: "[The New World] will bear away / The palm of greatness from the Eastern world" (p. 55). Latter-day military heroes such as Colonel Johnson of Emmons' *Tecumseh* and Robert Rogers of *Pontiac* fight for American liberty, justice and "equality sure enough" (Macomb, p. 22). Patriotism is associated not only with vision and heroism but also with spirituality and motherhood.

Oh! Love of Country! Passion of the Soul! Inherent in the human mind and heart, implanted by our mother's sacred loves, as points she to the heart of love and hope! It does not claim the city only, or the wild; it emanates from love maternal here, and rises from that parent to our God (Jones, p. 72).

Interestingly national loyalty was not claimed by or assigned to whites exclusively.[16] Jones' Tecumseh declaimed the above, and every tragic Indian hero would have concurred. "A tear is due to Logan... he outlived.... his nation" (Doddridge, p. 3). Metamora resolves "never ... to forsake the home of his father nor let the plough of strangers disturb the bones of his hushed" (Stone, p. 22), and he vows to live free or die: "Our nation's freedom! Or the Grave!" (p. 35). Pontiac lectures the English soldiers: "A red man knows his rights as well as a white man, and each ought to sustain them, for his country's honor and his own good name" (Macomb, p. 48). Pontiac's assassin justifies his act as "a sacrifice to our country's peace" (p. 55). In the introduction to *Tecumseh and the Prophet*, Jones instructs the reader that "no characteristic is more worthy of the admiration of a free people" (p. 1, Preface) than patriotism. His hero, whose name, according to Jones, translates as "falling star,"[17] compares himself with King Philip: "And When Tecumseh feels that his great fight / Is to be fought, if Victory be not here— / A Patriot's death awaits him mid the doom / Of his dear Country's fall" (p. 43). Country is dear to the Europeans as well. Adelaide of *Carabasset,* a play replete with displaced persons, rhapsodizes on her homeland, Acadie; Father Ralle from France suggests that the only passion stronger than the love of country is the love of God. Ratcliffe of Owen's Pocahontas leads a movement to return to England **and abandon the unprofitable settlement in this "drear and** howling wilderness" (Owen, p. 41).

American patriotism is inspired not only by the American heroes but also by the dramatized events from American history, events distant enough to be non-controversial but glorious enough to be stirring: the settlement of Jamestown, King Philip's War, Pontiac's Rebellion and the Battle of Tippecanoe, for example. The playwrights claim that these events are accurately portrayed. Doddridge describes *Logan* as "strictly correct in all its historical allusions" (p. 4); Deering says *Carabasset* is "founded on fact" (p. 3); Barker claims a "close adherence to truth" (p. 3); and Barnes asserts that "this tale is no fiction... it is historical in the most minute details" (p. 1). All the playwrights also deny any conflict between "historical" and "national," i.e., patriotic, and the prefaces reassure the reader that what follows is both glorifying and true to the utmost particular.[18]

Patriotism is also advanced by the celebration of American character, identified principally through repudiation, i.e., by constrast with the other, both Indian and European. Indian barbarism, meaning vengefulness, cruelty, lawlessness and paganism, is contrasted with American civilization, meaning knowledge, refinement, order and holy zeal for Christianity. Unlike the cruel and treacherous Indians, Americans, whether colonial or national, are merciful, honest and just. Unlike the false, pretentious and effete English, Americans are vigorous, brave, honorable, simple and egalitarian. They also know their way around: "You need not care much for the redcoats," advises Pontiac, "they know **nothing of the woods, but the blue jackets [Americans] are old** enemies of ours and know what they are all about" (Macomb, p. 41). The American is more heroic in battle than his English counterpart, and he lives more courageously in the perilous wilderness. Unlike the typical English characters Mordaunt, in *Metamora*, and Roland and Edith, in *Nick of the Woods*, he is not haunted by the past, and in some cases, such as Walter in *Metamora* or George in *The Octoroon*, he appears to be fatherless.[19] Unlike the English, French and Indians, Americans are portrayed as innocent, simple, merciful, natural egalitarians who are self-respecting, heroic, independent and patriotic. If not pious, they are at least God-fearing Protestants, whose hearts are "busting up with freedom, truth and right."

This "splendid juggernaut" of patriotism, however, does not run smoothly or uninterruptedly; the way is rough with inconsistencies and contradictions. Apart from imputed cruelty and paganism, the noble native Americans and the Anglo-Europeans share the same values and virtues. Both are brave in battle, both protect their women and children. Both are willing to sacrifice themselves for their countries, and both are dedicated to freedom and equality. It is hard to distinguish Tecumseh from General Harrison or Colonel Johnson from Pontiac or Powhatan from Smith.[20]

Jingoistic patriotism, moreover, exists side-by-side with severe criticism,[21] especially of Indian affairs. The criticism is uttered by red and white alike and usually is confirmed by the action of the play. Apart from *Nick of the Woods* and *The Octoroon*, the accusation of and conviction for injustice against the Indian by whites is constant. The Indians are justifiably amazed and outraged at the fundamental, progressive immorality of the white's treatment. Despite the

original "hearty welcome" found in the wigwams, and despite
the debt incurred by the settlers who would not have survived
without Indian aid— "the red man took you in as a little
child and opened the door of his wigwam" (Stone, p. 22)—
whites steal, lie, murder and debase their ally. In Owen's
Pocahontas, Utta urges Powhatan to dispel the trespassers,
the "Longknives":

They first asked just to land—then for shelter for the sick; they couldn't leave,
and asked to put up shelters. In the spring they put up their guns and said they
wouldn't leave. Now they demand food and pillage our store houses and fire on
our sacred Okee (p. 81).

Utta accurately predicts that the Longknives will pull down
their common house and put out the tribal fire with the blood
"of those who received them in peace and kindness" (p. 83).
Utta's prophecy is realized in *Logan*. The chief and his father
have befriended and succored the whites, yet, the beholden
have slaughtered all Logan's unprotected tribe without
provocation.

I appeal to any white man to say, if ever he entered Logan's cabin hungry, and
he gave him not meat; if ever he came cold and naked, and he clothed him not.
During the course of the last long and bloody war Logan remained idle in his
cabin, an advocate for peace. Such was my love for the whites, that my
countrymen pointed as they passed, and said, 'Logan is the friend of the white
men.' I had even thought to have lived with you, but for the injuries of one man.
Colonel Cresap, the last spring, in cold blood, and unprovoked, murdered all
relations of Logan, not even sparing my women and children. There runs not a
drop of my blood in the veins of any living creature. Who is there to mourn for
Logan?[22]

Metamora also characterizes the supplicants as insufferable
marauders. "Thou are a white man, and thy veins hold the
blood of a robber" (p. 36). The whites also murder the innocent,
deceive the trusting and misuse Indian women. as Owen's
Smith predicts, the Christians have taught the "heathen"
cruelty, infidelity, immorality and deceit (p. 191).

   The teachers are motivated by greed, "the fiend of
palefaces" (Jones, p. 78): "Avarice combined with power,
stretched forth its iron hand, and dashed them [the Indians]

off" (Deering, p. 19). "Yet such is the ambition of the paleface in his suppos'd-yet weak, uncertain pow'r, that he could e'en the constant North-Star grasp... no thought to purify the spirit here, does he give—Av'rice blinds him down to earth" (Jones, p. 91).

The whites are not only greedy but unjust. They violate one another's rights, substantiating Tecumseh's charge that "Laws were indeed required for the Pale face; his oft committed crimes and injuries on others' rights prove their necessity" (p. 38). Smith has not only to survive the hostility of the savages, but also to protect himself from the perfidy of other colonists, commoner and aristocrat alike. The warfare and animosity among the British, Americans and French is incipient or actual throughout. Protestants and Catholics bear each other as much malice as Indians and settlers. Metamora, speaking of Roger Williams' banishment from Massachusetts Bay Colony, ponders on the religious intolerance of his prosecutors:

Why was that man sent away from the house of his joy? Because the Great Spirit did not speak to him as he had spoken to you? Did you not come across the great waters and leave the smoke of your father's hearth because the iron hand was held out against you and your hearts were sorrowful in the high places of prayer? Why do you that have just plucked the red knife from your own wounded sides, strive to stab your brother? (Stone, p. 21).

Powhatan is also impressed by the fratricide: "The red man wars with strangers, enemies; but thou would'st slay thy brothers" (Barnes, p. 205). And Pontiac and Matacoran pose the question of loyalty that haunts many of these plays: "How comes it that you should invade these distant regions, and leave a country and a King you delight so much to praise" (Macomb, p. 19), and "if you English so love your own country, why cross the wide sea to deprive the poor Indian of his rude and savage forests?" (Custis, p. 189).

Loyalty and betrayal are at issue in many relationships— between God and mortals; kings and subjects; master and servant; parent and child; husband and wife; brother and sister; friends. Throughout these dramas the writers' interest in all the relationships is first and foremost with the matter of loyalty. *Metamora* is a typical case. In the opening scene, Mordaunt, the unsuspected regicide, calls to "England, my home! When will thy parent arms enfold me?" (Stone, p. 9). Next, his daughter, Oceana, is seen calling upon her deceased parent, who has symbolically deserted her, "to forget me not" (p. 10). "Dear Walter," her lover, appears and complains that he has no known father and is nameless and poor. Directly thereafter Metamora, King of the Wampanoags, who refers to himself as "The Father" of his people and the adopted **Kaweshine, and who acts as father to the priest Annawandah** and is shown as a devoted father to an infant son, appears. He **speaks reverently of his heroic father, Massasoit, who acted as** a father to the Pilgrims, and then gives paternal advice to Oceana and Walter. In the next scene, Fitzarnold, the aristocratic suitor to Oceana, who can protect Mordaunt from reprisal and exposure, comes to claim his bride, and the question of Oceana's loyalty to her father is raised. Shall she do as bidden and marry the profligate or follow her own inclinations and wed the hapless Walter? Thereafter Errington, pompous chief of the Puritan council, is introduced as "Our council's father," although his authority is later challenged. Metamora critiizes him for expelling Roger Williams and being untrue to their spiritual father. Metamora's prophet, Kaweshine, predicts that the Great Spirit will desert his red children. Kaweshine, Annawandah, Puritans and the Narragansetts betray Philip. Nahmeokee's father is betrayed by King Uncas. At the end, Metamora kills Fitzarnold, rescuing Oceana as an honorable father might have. He also kills the traitorous Annawandah. A former, faithless servant of Sir Arthur Vaughn's, who has transferred his loyalty to Fitzarnold and who is urged to faithfulness to his master by the spotless Walter, reveals that Walter is Vaughn's son. Later King Philip dies on his fathers' "throne," true to his oath: "Never will Metamora forsake the home of his fathers" (Stone, p. 21)

This preoccupation with filial and civic fidelity in these popular plays dealing with national character, identity and destiny suggests a substratum of psychic meaning. One approach to the subliminal import, considered at greater length in Chapter 5, is to consider what psychic needs of the audience were being met by the filial myths of these plays, whose widespread and enduring success over more than twenty-five years attests to their mythic ministration.

The pre-and post-revolutionary American feeling that the British king was or had been the legitimate father of his subjects has been substantiated by Winthrop Jordan,[23] and Edwin Burrows and Michael Wallace.[24] That the Revolution constituted a rejection of the symbolic father has been argued by Geoffrey Goren,[25] Richard Slotkin, Frederic Crews,[26] Leslie Fiedler and others. Paul Nagel in *This Sacred Trust* presents a profusion of quotations from contemporary orations, sermons, newspapers, books, hymns, magazines, letters and diaries and convincingly concludes that particularly during the period 1815-1848 Americans struggled to reconcile the lofty calling of the nation established by the founding fathers with the meager attainments of the sons.

As Lawrence J. Friedman (*Inventors of the Promised Land*, p. 2) points out, "God's chosen people had not performed their mission; they seemed destined for eternal perdition." This struggle was often cast in familial imagery. The fathers had established an invaluable inheritance of republicanism and morality. The sons' responsibility was to guard the fathers' work: to kneel in humble adoration "at the lofty vestibule"[27] of the fathers' shrine. Daniel Webster argued that the nation's identity, "the dear purchase of our fathers" (p. 8), was a "sacred trust" for all the sons to come. Yet, as Michael Paul Rogin points out, "They [the fathers] bequeathed an ambiguous heritage...[and] the sons lived in the shadow.... [They] contrasted their own materialism unfavorably with the public spirit of the fathers" (pp. 14-15).

The symbolic patricide in the American psyche between the Revolution and the end of the Jacksonian Era generated guilt which was expressed in imaginative literature at large. Frederic Crews, for example, has traced Hawthorne's obsessive concern with fathers and sons to a sense of guilt and a fear of retribution. It is also clear in the language of rational thought. Thomas Jefferson typically deplored the "unwise and unworthy passion of...sons" (Nagel, p. 77) and orators threatened the citizenry with doom unless they returned to "the holy spirit of our ancestors" (Nagel, p. 10).

The Indian dramas not only reflect this guilt and anxiety, they also absolve it. The treatment afforded fathers tends to exculpate rebellious sons and to alleviate filial guilt and anxiety. In all the Pocahontas plays, *Metamora, Octoroon, Oolaita* and *Nick of the Woods*, fathers fail and are discredited. Mordaunt, the regicide in *Metamora*, tries to gain immunity from punishment by forcing his daughter to marry an English profligate. Metamora's deceased father, who urges his son by signs to fight the English, is responsible for the extinction of the race. Pocahontas' father, Powhatan, is represented as cruel, superstitious and devious in all the plays, and the audience is prompted to rejoice at Pocahontas' rejection of him and his ways. Oolaita's father's insensitive tyranny causes his daughter's death, and the disapproving fathers of the newly-weds are responsible for forcing their children into the perilous situation in the Lakota wildwood. In *The Octoroon* the father figure has so misjudged his family and friends and so mismanaged his affairs that his illegitimate octoroon daughter is threatened with enslavement, his widow with bankruptcy and indigence, and his nephew with marriage to an unloved woman. The denial of fathers also serves to relieve that guilt. Walter of *Metamora* is ostensibly an orphan;[28] the eloquent Tecumseh rhapsodizes about his mother but never **speaks of his father; George, the young hero of *The Octoroon*,** has been raised by a deceased uncle; Adelaide, the pure white vessel of *Carabasset*, is fatherless, as is the heroic Telie in *Nick of the Woods*. In every play, the Indians are presented as true to their fathers and pious toward ancestors, and in every play, they are defeated. The message is that unjust or unwise fathers do not deserve the respect and loyalty of their children. In fact, it is the latter's duty to society and to self to overthrow the malevolent despots.

Guilt is also mitigated through the opposite techniques: apotheosis of fathers, the celebration of filial fidelity and the vilification of perfidy. Captain John Smith, General William Henry Harrison, Colonel Rogers of Rogers' Rangers, George Washington, and other official Great Fathers are treated as heroes and saints: "In such a cause, 'tis sweet to die and saint your name with Washington on high" (Emmons, p. 33). Loyalty and obedience to the father and the fatherland are qualities assigned to the heroes,[29] red and white alike, although more consistently and intensely to the Indians, and the effects of perfidy and rebellion are often presented as destructive. In *Metamora* Mordaunt's regicide is treated as an unnatural abomination and prepares the audience for his unnatural willingness to sacrifice his child to save himself. The treachery of Sir Arthur Vaughn's servant has caused his master and Walter to suffer separation; the faithless Annawandah and the desertion of Ayantic and the Mohicans are partly responsible for the Wampanoag's extermination; the disobedience of Kaweshine results in Philip's death. The villains of both races are disloyal. Jones' heroic Tecumseh is brought low by his brother and the seditious Winnemac; Emmons' Tecumseh is betrayed by General Proctor, his English ally. In Barnes' *Forest Princess*, both Powhatan and Smith are deceived by the ambitious Volday, who later falsely and unsuccessfully accuses Rolfe of treason to the King. In Owen's version, Ratcliffe sends Smith deep into Indian territory, hoping the savages will do his dirty work, while other settlers plan to seize a ship and abandon their follow colonists in this "grave of Europeans" (p. 49). The Indian villains also plot against their leaders. Pontiac is assassinated by Augushaway; the merciless Monona of *Oolaita* disobeys his king and tries to murder his countryman Tallula, thereby causing the death of Oolaita; the perfidious Ravillac of *Carabasset* betrays his foster father, Ralle, which causes the father's death as well as the extinction of the Norridgewok tribe. Even comic figures, such as Robin in Barker's *Indian Princess,* take up the theme in playful attempts at cuckoldry.

Most importantly, Americans are portrayed as faithful to the Father in Heaven. They accept their roles in the realization of Manifest Destiny and thereby show themselves as true, innocent and faithful sons of the Great Father: "Adams all / Before the Fall."

The images and mythologies of the Indian dramas ostensibly provide a factual account of historical events, a true depiction of individual personalities, and a reliable representation of entire races and cultures. Actually, they provide what Melville in *The Confidence Man* called the "metaphysics of Indian hating": a way of perceiving and evaluating history that vindicates the whites.[30] Beneath the glossed surface of dramatized rationalization, however, is the turbulent energy and confusion of guilt.

The exoneration from this guilt is achieved by various means. The Indian is first dehumanized and depersonalized by **stereotyped and formulaic characterization. He is also vilified** and provides a savage measure of civilization; that is, whites identify themselves as the superior non-savage: the merciful, the just, the honest, the peaceful, the enlightened, the innocent. Even the most elevated of the four wooden figures, the noble **savage, serves these purposes.**[31] **Although he is eloquent,** honorable, intelligent and the best of his race, he is also the last, which means he is no match for the whites, even if the latter is comic and simple. Moreover, his wax-museum greatness is always qualified by his cruelty, ignorance and heathenism, which he shares with the horror-show Indian, the savage with a heart and mind of darkness, who certainly deserves the extermination he gets. This subhuman Indian, who is represented as more racially typical, was as useful to the apologists as that cigar-store Indian was to the tobacconist. The third Indian, who is subdued and acculturated, is portrayed as either a drunken nuisance or criminal, a sort of destroyed savage Semele unto whom the glorious, but fatal, laws of civilization have appeared; or as an exotic Step-and-Fetch-It. He represents the results of white-red contact. There can be no peaceful co-existence—the uncompromising nobleman dies and the surviving compromiser is debased. Once eloquent, he becomes unintellible; once racially pure, he ends a "mish-mash" of French, Mexican and Indian;[32] once rational and commanding, he is now drunk; once exemplary, now despicable; once a protector, now a murderer; once a sire of champions, now'a latent homosexual or eunuch. Once he held the graves of his fathers to be sacred; now he is often a traitor to his people. This castrated red man is equivalent to the Indian woman, that "rare wench," who deserts her family, betrays her lover, abandons her race, rejects her culture, blasphemes against her religion and risks her life, as well as her identity, because of the white man's potency—sexual, technological, supernatural. She serves him as lover and mother; she satisfies his lust and also defends him, while maintaining her independence and allowing him perfect freedom. Yet she too is made inferior and savage by her ignorance, her eroticism and her dark complexion.

The plots limit these four Indians to three possibilities: co-habitation and acculturation; "light[ing] out for the territory," thereby postponing the encounter; or defying the whites and dying: "Civilization or death." The plots always feature both races (none of these plays deals exclusively with Indians) in an encounter that is generally hostile. The dramatized battles usually show the Indian as aggressor and always as loser. His losses are accounted for by American military technology and skill, the treachery of fellow tribesmen, and the will of God.

The literary form that best accommodated the myths of the Vanishing American and Manifest Destiny was a synthesis of melodrama and tragedy. Most plays feature an abundance of Indian spectacles, thrilling action, despicable villains, "good and godlike" white heroes (Barker, p. 603), and sometimes an Indian hero whose cruel fate and suffering are made meaningful and tolerable through his savagery and God's inscrutable Providence, which decrees the white man's triumph and sanctifies building a society on Indian graves.

Yet the plays contradict and betray themselves, and recall D.H. Lawrence's charge of duplicity against American literature.[33] Despite a strident, spread-eagle patriotism, the plays sharply criticize American avarice, treachery and indecency, not only against the Indian but against one another. Although the Indian is defiled by imputation, he is often the incarnate complex of virtues that the plays praise.[33] Although loyalty to fathers and the fatherland is celebrated, fathers are systematically discredited and denied, and rebellious sons are excused. Indeed, betrayal is the secret or subliminal theme of most of the "national dramas," which themselves betray a sense of guilt that is not quite quieted by the telling of tales or guilded by the mythological glory.

Chapter 5

The land! Don't you feel it? Doesn't it make you want to go out and lift dead Indians tenderly from their graves, to steal from them—as if it must be clinging even to their corpses—some authenticity....

William Carlos Williams, *In The American Grain*
(New York: New Directions Paperback, 1956, p. 74)

"The anxiety quotient has always been abnormally high in American history," writes Page Smith, "and it may even distinguish Americans from all other people in history."[1] Ralph Waldo Emerson, in a lecture printed in *The Dial* a century earlier, observed, "I question whether doubt and care ever wrote their names so legibly on the face of any population."[2] The American experience, colonial as well as national, present as well as past, has given rise to intense guilt and anxiety.

From the outset, anxiety was inherent in the American situation. The Puritans immigrated to a fearsome, lonely wilderness to execute the awesome responsibility of establishing a unique Christian commonwealth, a City upon a Hill, a model for the reform of all Christendom. Initially they expected that failure to build a Bible commonwealth would prompt divine vengeance:

The Lord will surely break out in wrath against us... and be revenged against such a perjured people and make us know the price of the break of such a covenant... for we must consider that... the eyes of all people are upon us; so that if we shall deal falsely with our God in this work we have undertaken and so cause him to withdraw his present help from us, we shall be made a story and a byword through the world.[3]

Individually as well as collectively, they lived in doubt. Had God extended His grace to them? Had their conversion experience been genuine? Were they truly chosen or hopelessly damned? Moreover, as Winthrop Jordon and others have pointed out, by rejecting the fatherland and the authority of the established church, they knew the patricidal guilt of succeeding revolutionists who overthrew the King. Furthermore the several generations after the Revolution were confronted with the complexities of building a glorious national identity and destiny despite this heritage of guilt, which was compounded by the failure to make significant progress toward the Founding Fathers' ideals. The latter failure, as Paul Nagel notes, produced widespread anxiety and despair, which was at least as common as the vigorous optimism usually attributed to this period. Lawrence Friedman characterizes the period as a "time of trouble" marked by "chronic inner apprehensions" (p. 2).

The political climate of the latter period, as one would expect, was unstable. David H. Fischer[4] has established that the unity and deference of the Age of Founding Fathers was over, and the elite government was collapsing. "Political parties were replacing filial deference as an ordering principle" (p. 12). Mob rule and leadership by what some called "odious reptiles" was feared. The country was bitterly divided by political and regional interests.

Under the circumstances, a collective national identity was complicated and threatened by the moral austerity required of patriots in a country which believed in the divine superintendence of its glorious destiny. "If America accepts God's design, it might lead mankind to the greatest victory and felicity that humanity can hope to attain" (Nagel, p. 104). Nonetheless this "nation with the soul of the church," as G.K. Chesterton once called it, was adopting unhallowed policies toward native peoples, condoning the enslavement of fellow human beings and devoting itself to the attainment of worldly goods and powers. "Commerce, trade, and stocks," said James Russell Lowell later when the commercial spirit had become even more pervasive, "are our religion."[5]

Nonetheless Americans concomitantly persisted in the early nineteenth century in also conceiving of themselves as prelapsarian Adams without history or sin. They imagined themselves Stewards in the Vineyards of the Lord, charged with the dutiful, strict performance of moral and sacred duties for God and country. Nationality, it was said, depended on each citizen's struggle with evil. It became increasingly obvious during this period, nonetheless, that Americans, the "chosen people," although "freighted with the hopes of humanity" (Nagel, p. 60), were as subject as the rest of the human species to greed, passion and self-interest. Noah Webster concluded that the Sacred Trust, the mandate to prove that republican government could sustain both liberty and order, was beyond the capacity of the Stewards. "We deserve **all our public evils. We are a degenerate and wicked people.**"[6]

Other conditions contributed to the despair. No stability was provided by class or office or occupation, and change was so fast that Americans had to move ever more quickly. "We have St. Vitus dance,"[7] Thoreau observed. Unprecedented industrial growth, the fast pace of urbanization of an agricultural society, the political tumult of the Jacksonian era, the decline of religion and the rise of secularism, the romantic awareness of man's duality, and the decline of family order, helped to shatter the American sense of reality. The prevailing myths became suspect, and they could no longer buttress the authority of the church, the state, the father or the mind. National experience was either disqualifying or modifying the traditional stories as models for imitation and as credible metaphors explaining that national experience and identity. As earlier certainties became disputable, visions failed and chaos threatened.

An urgent search for national definition of the real, the true and the good ensued in many forms: there was a resurgence of revivalism and evangelical religion and Utopian communities; a reassertion of belief in America's partnership with Providence in the form of the doctrine of Manifest Destiny; a conservatism that identified true Americanism with ancestor worship; and a consoling insistence that American character and achievement lay in the future.

The uneasy psychological climate also produced a readiness to "transform experience, perception, and narration into a myth ... a process of reasoning by metaphor in which direct statement and logical analysis are replaced by figurative and poetic statement" (Slotkin, p. 7). This readiness was expressed during the first half of the nineteenth century in demands for a genuine, indigenous American literature, independent of European influences, glorifying American achievements, disclosing American meaning and serving to unify the American people. In effect, an American mythology was called for. The demands did not go unheeded. Unprecedented literary activity in various genres and styles was generated. Irving's *Sketch Book* was published in 1819, and shortly thereafter Cooper's *Spy* and Dana's *Idle Man*. Along with these figures came a host of other writers including William Cullen Bryant, Joseph Rodman Drake, James Gates Percival, Robert Montgomery Bird, Catharine Sedgwick and later, of course, Emerson, Thoreau, Hawthorne, Poe and Melville—all within a period of roughly thirty years. It was also during this period that the American Indian dramas, concerned with the justification and glorification of American identity and destiny, were written and performed.

It will be useful to consider in more detail the anxieties that characterized the first half of the nineteenth century and to identify the varied attempts to achieve mythic resolution or alleviation of those anxieties, particularly through the Indian Dramas.

During the Jacksonian era, many Americans were questioning their own sense of reality and worth. What had seemed certain and fixed had become doubtful and unreliable. The colonial and European myths and images which had structured American experience were no longer entirely credible. Inasmuch as "processes of perception and conception, organizing and understanding the signs that come... in our dialogue with the circumambient world are guided and formed by images in our mind,"[8] the sense of loss and confusion and despair was keen.

The "circumambient world," was in flux. Changing of institutional, environmental and philosophical conditions **was negating the viability of the myths Americans had briefly** lived by. The only generally recognized political authority had been rejected during the Revolution. Rogin points out that during the Jacksonian era the family order, which was perceived as a model of American virtue, was giving way to possessive individualism through the workings of commodity capitalism (pp. 7-10). Philosophical views about man and his relationship to other men and to the universe were revolutionized. Further, the institutions of American culture— the government, the church, the university, the family and the economic organization—were also changing rapidly, and they were unable to inculcate a firm new sense of cultural reality.[9] They could not confirm old stories or prompt viable replacements, having lost whatever imaginative authority they once had.

The spokesmen for these institutions were outstanding among the orators who expressed doubt and despair about the old truths of American life.[10] By 1824 Thomas Jefferson, one of the "national officers instructed with the oracle of Eternal Truth" (Nagel, p. 20), had passed from optimistic belief in the **republic, expressed in his first inaugural remarks, as "the** world's best hope,"[11] to a hopeless despair: "I regret that I am now to die in the belief that the useless sacrifice of themselves by the generation of 1776, to acquire self-government and happiness to their country, is to be thrown away by the unwise and unworthy passions of their sons" (p. 614). Despite his earlier optimism about American destiny, by 1833, Henry Clay began to recoil at the anarchy, violence and despotism he foresaw, and by 1832, he thought the country was in grave peril. "No one can discern any termination of this sad state of things [national corruption], nor see in the future any glimpse of light or hope."[12] Abraham Lincoln, in 1838, responding to widespread despair and guilt about American destiny and character, acknowledged his doubt about the "noble experiment": "If destruction be our lot," he said, it was due to the "wild and furious passions" of the citizenry.[13] Violence and emotion were "common to the whole country" (p. 93). If the nation was to survive and progress, Lincoln said, every citizen must "swear by the blood of the Revolution" (p. 93) to revere the law. Emerson expressed doubt that America could fulfill the world's hopes as a model republic and connected this with the absence of a pillar of fire to follow: "Is there no venerable tradition whose genuineness and authority we can establish, or must we too hurry onward, inglorious in ignorance and misery we know not whence, we know not whither."[14] Quentin Anderson comments on this misery in the generation after Jefferson's: "Americans appear to have suffered a punishing psychic blow in the generation of Emerson's youth... to have lost the assurance provided by the presence of leaders and an institutional order.... There was an acute and widely diffuse emotional demand for a new mode of self-validation, a search for authority" (pp. 234, 236).

The "venerable traditions" of the past were more intimidating than assuring. The West had long been imagined by the European mind as a realm of freedom and a kind of paradise—the Isles of the Blest or Elysium or the Hesperides.[15] Columbus imagined that he might have discovered the Earthly Paradise itself. The Puritans also conceived of the New World as a potential Promised Land, dependent upon the success of their "errand into the wilderness." It was a second chance for mankind to live according to the Word of God—to create an American Canaan. Both colonials and nationals regarded the New World as a fruitful garden in which mankind's ability to reconcile freedom with social order and personal morality and happiness could be proven.[16] America, according to the poet Joel Barlow, was both a depository and a guardian of mankind's best interests: a "sacred deposit."[17] America could triumph "if we accept God's design," but failure "would blast the hopes of the friends of liberty... throughout the world, to the end of time" (Nagel, p. 59). On the outcome of the American endeavor rested "the civilization of the earth, the reform of the governments of the ancient world, and the emancipation of the whole race" (p. 60).

Individual citizens were responsible for the fulfillment of these awesome national goals. This meant that national work was "to combat sin" (p. 111). Citizens acknowledged that "Providence, in the peculiar circumstances in which it has

placed us, in the free institutions it has given us, has made it
our duty to bring out the ideal man" (p. 61). Senator Asher
Robbins testified that never before had a people emerged
"whose private virtues were a substitute for government
itself—and a sufficient substitute" (p. 111).

The actualities of American experience and of human
nature soon qualified these myths as reassuring truths and
"venerable traditions" about American destiny, character,
capability, and the American alliance with the divine. Instead
of "becoming an example for the imitation of the whole world,"
as James K. Polk had prophesied, America had become an
object of scorn and derision to many of her own citizens. They
described her as a materialistic, divided, violent, undisciplined
nation, "carrying patriotism to market and principle to the
devil" (p. 122). Millard Fillmore prayed for those "most favored
people" who had been expected to realize utopian national
ideals: "May God save the people; for it is evident the people
will not."[18] Aristabulus Bragg in Cooper's *Home as Found*,
who was "ready to turn out not only his hand but his heart and
his principles, to anything that offers an advantage"[19] became
as common in the contemporary imagination as the sober,
selfless Steward laboring in the Lord's Vineyard. It was said
again that God would punish in wrath this impenitent and
wayward nation. John H. Rice, a professor in the Virginia
Union Theological School, wrote an essay in 1828 entitled "The
Power of Love," predicting like Winthrop, that should America
fail to reveal... "the city of God built up, in all its beauty and
glory," the penalty would be frightful. "Heavy indeed would...
be our reckoning, and terrible the visitation of justice....."[20] The
Panic of 1837, some wrote, was divine retribution for America's
failure to fulfill her part of the contract with Providence. The
betrayal of national, and thus religious, commitments seemed
so great to some millenialist sects, such as the Millerites, that
they prepared for the Day of Judgment, disposing of all
property except ascension robes. Since it was widely held that
the relationship between "politics and religion is like that of
the body and the soul" (Nagel, p. 13), many politicians urged
national repentance.[21] It was proposed that July 4 be made a

religious holiday observed by church services and prayer meetings. John Adams said that the nation was sorely afflicted because it had sinned mightily, and he recommended that America confess before God and hope that the humiliation would foster a renewed spirit of Christian kinship.[22] God's chosen people, as Lawrence Friedman points out, "had not performed their mission; they seemed destined for eternal perdition" (p. 2).

The American mythological responses to other theological questions were also in flux.[23] Institutionalized religion was declining. The conventional churches of the Jacksonian era had become increasingly unpopular, and the broad faiths of Unitarians and transcendentalism lacked clear doctrines[24] and conventional religious appeal. The basic patriarchal myth of the Puritan God as a demanding father who presided over a church of fathers, was challenged. By 1829 William Ellery Channing deplored "subjection to Deity... to mere power and will, as anything but virtue."[25]

The church-sanctioned myths of woman as Eve, as feeling easily seduced by evil, a seducer of Reason herself, and as temptation to sin, were being replaced by the myth of woman as an immaculate and innocent savior.[26] In this repressed era the church, as well as all other institutions, failed to provide mythological models for the solution of complex sexual problems. Leslie Fiedler observes that the Puritan divine would not have been as shocked as Henry Thoreau at the phallic forms in nature (p. 81), nor, one might add, as offended as Nathaniel Hawthorne by undraped Roman statuary.

In addition to the political, industrial and religious revolutions, the conception of the human mind was radically transformed during this time. As Leslie Fiedler points out, the awareness of the mind's antagonistic duality, its subconscious as well as conscious element, led to a new conception of the self as "double to the final depths,"[27] and sanctioned revolutionary reversals: whatever had been suspect, outcast, and denied is **postulated as good "...Patricides become the objects of veneration.... Before [now] no one...had doubted the** inferiority of passion to reason, of impulse to law."[28] This "libidinal breakthrough" (p. xxx) was what Quentin Anderson calls "a sky-sweeping operation." By the 1840s America had produced Henry Thoreau who questioned all authority but his own, prescribed renunciation of convention and tradition, regretted his "goodness" and lamented: "What demon possessed me that I behaved so well."[29]

Yet from another point of view, this revolutionary tendency was inherent in the American experience. America had been challenging authority from the beginning. The discovery and settlement of the country and the founding of the nation had been predicated upon the revolutionary assumption that escape from culture and the past and authority could mean happiness as well as freedom. Fiedler observes: "There is... something blasphemous in the very act by which America was established, a gesture of defiance that began with the symbolic breaching of the pillars of Hercules long considered the divine sign of limit."[30] The up-starts persisted in the blasphemy, defying Church, King, Old World standards, customs and fealty, as well as the anxious European relatives who discouraged emigration. Michael Paul Rogin adds that "The new American world undermined the authority provided by history, tradition, family connection, and the other ties of old European existence" (p. 9). Denial and protest seemed an American mode. Henry James observed that "Democracy is born of denial... and destruction. It comes into existence in the way of denying established institutions."[31] During the period under consideration the urge to remove all traces of the Old World became so intense that some regretted that Americans had to communicate with one another in an inherited language. Americans were urged to reject every existing mode of organizing and explaining experience, to confront life in entirely original terms, to establish, as Emerson said, "an original relation with the universe." This psychology of separation was perpetuated by the influx of immigrants and exiles who themselves had abandoned home and country and broken the family circle. They too had left native traditions, values and myths. They had trained their children to accept alien myths and values, to speak a new language, and to be loyal to new laws. In this "one generation culture,"[32] the failure of fathers as Quentin Anderson phrases it, and the betrayal of fathers is inevitable and perpetual.

The actual unhappiness, guilt and anxiety that resulted from the challenge to mythological, political and familial authority were pronounced during the rapid shifts of the Jacksonian era. The "son of man" had come to dwell in "a rebellious house." The usual modes of finding authority and establishing a relationship with it were complicated since old authorities were being discredited by the realities of the time and widely accepted new authorities had not yet been established. Americans were experiencing some of the anticipated exhilaration of freedom, but they were also aware of a profound national guilt coupled with fear and insecurity, caused by the defiance or loss of authorities through political revolutions and mythical discontinuity or disintegration. To betray or defy fathers was to create a vast, cosmic vacuum which resulted in a sense of nothingness, meaninglessness and arbitrariness. It was also to know the guilt of the patricide and the anxiety of the wrong-doer who anticipates revenge. The happiness-freedom equation was obviously but a half truth. Writing about his countrymen in a letter in 1822, Emerson noted that "too much knowledge and too much liberty makes them mad" (Rusk, p. 245). The "non serviam" motto did seem to lead to Hell.

The "madness" lead to a frenetic search for national authority. Although, as Emerson asserted, the Jacksonian era was distinguished by "the refusal of Authority,"[33] it was also characterized by a search for new, American authorities[34] or to reconciliation with old ones. National guilt was assuaged by "devotion to patrimony" (Nagel, p. 10), as Daniel Webster recommended for the "evil times" of the 1830s. "True Americanism is ancester worship," declared Samuel Knapp, popular orator and biographer of Daniel Webster. "The light shining on one ancient grave will reach another, until the commingled radiance will form a pillar of fire to guide us through every night of danger that may come upon our nation."[35] "The Fathers have left us nothing to achieve," confessed Daniel Webster like a repentant son. "We had only to preserve uninpaired what they had achieved for us" (Nagel, p. 89).[36]

Others affirmed the English patrimony, which not only established authority but also conciliated the offended symbolic parent. Horace Bushnell warned a Yale audience in 1837 that national survival depended upon acceptance of English heritage and Saxon design: "Piety to God and to ancestors are the only force which can impart an organic unity and vitality to a state. Torn from the past and from God, government is but a dead and brute machine" (Nagel, p. 68). *The New York Review* countered objections to reunion with England: "We can see no difficulty in preserving a pure and lofty tone of American nationality together with an affectionate reverence for the time-honored country of our forefathers."[37]

There were other pleas to restore God the Father to His Heaven and His authority. Calls for patriotic renewals of faith in Providence and a return to Christian morality came from the halls of Congress, from revival tents, and from sailing vessels from which Evangelists performed God's missionary work by Americanizing the world. Ministers and presidents, editors and educators, ecclesiastics and scholars deplored American corruption by wealth and luxury and power. They predicted that should the depraved Stewards continue to live in transgression of divine purpose, the Union would not be preserved: "Thus Endeth the Nation that Despised the Lord **and Gloried in Wisdom, Wealth, and Power**" (Nagel, p. 115), prophesied Lyman Beecher, writing in the *Nation Preacher*, a magazine that warned that America's only hope was to surrender herself to God (p. 114). Orestes Brownson urged Americans to "return to God, put our trust in Him, and live for the end to which He has appointed us."[38] Horace Mann contended that "Moral education is a primal necessity of social existence... and a community without a conscience would soon extinguish itself."[39]

From the beginning America had been both a "community with a conscience" and a community with a divine destiny.

Christian imperialism had justified the colonization of Virginia: "God in his wisdom... [had] enriched the savage countries, that those riches might be attractive for Christian settlers, which there may sowe spirituals and reape temporals."[10] The Massachusetts Bay Colony had prospered with God's help. According to John Winthrop, God visited the smallpox epidemic upon the Indians so that the colonists could secure the country.[41] "The Manifest Destiny of providence in regard to the occupation of this continent" (Nagel, p. 107) was within the American "venerable tradition" of "surrender[ing] herself to God" (Nagel, p. 149).

Asserting the divine ordination of American history consecrated it and absolved the guilt and anxiety incurred by the defiance of earthly fathers.[42] Moreover, contemporary social issues such as exacerbated partisanship, rivalry of the three branches of government, laissez-faire capitalism and Indian policies seemed to be pre-ordained, and Americans but instruments of an implacable design and irrevocable necessity. In 1833, Timothy Flint, a Massachusetts missionary, invoked Manifest Destiny to justify the injustice and cruelty of Indian policies:

In the unchangeable order of things, two such races cannot exist together, each preserving its co-ordinate identity. Either this great continent, in the order of Providence should have remained in the occupancy of half a million of savages, engaged in everlasting conflicts of their peculiar warfare with each other, or it must have become, as it has, the domain of civilized millions. It is vain to charge upon the latter race results, which grew out of the laws of nature, and a universal march of human events.[43]

This impersonal dynamism meant that the nation had no control: "Of what avail will be our puny arm in rolling back the torrent of intellectual ideas and human progress, scooping their way along the steep of centuries?" (Nagel, p. 67).

The concept of divine destiny also meant that the realization of American character and achievement could be postponed to the future. Momentum toward a mysterious

Providential end was sufficient. "America is the Country of the Future," wrote Emerson in *The Dial* in 1844. "It is a country of beginnings, of projects, of vast designs, and expectations. It has no past: all has an outward and progressive look." Henry Thoreau concluded *Walden*, a book replete with ritual purgations or "busks" for guilt, by assuring the reader that the best is yet to be: "There is more day to dawn. The sun is but a morning star" (p. 266).

The search for authority and certainty and for "a pillar of fire to guide us through every night" led not only to God and country, but also to the replacement of conventional social authorities, and the institutions and mythologies that supported them, with what Quentin Anderson calls "The Imperial Self."[44] Emerson was the outstanding spokesman of this *causa sui* philosophy that postulated the distinctive, genuine individual as "possessed of the power to dispose of the whole felt and imagined world as a woman arranges her skirt" (Anderson, p. 55). The individual becomes a secular incarnation, taking the powers of the sacred and secular father and the customs and institutions of society into itself. Especially in his early career, Emerson followed the advice he had offered by the end of "Nature:" "Build therefore your own world" by creating for himself a world without death, fear or pain—a daytime world without the "night time facts." His world is not plural, intractable, arbitrary and evil because it was subject to the imaginative ordering of the primary, self-sufficient, transcendent individual consciousness.

The popularity of Emerson's philosophy, Anderson **argues, suggests that there was a "vast vacancy where fathers** had been"[45] and that "many Americans were attempting the emotional task... of incorporating [within themselves] the powers of the father who no longer seemed to be present, *qua* father, or minister, or state" (p. 55). Father or like figures of authority had never been as strong in America as they were in Europe. "Uncle Sam" was outside the immediate family circle, and, as Anderson asserts, there never had been a strong national consciousness or collective identity or life. But the absence of authority was keenly experienced during this period of post-revolutionary guilt and rapid economic, political and social shifts, and Emerson provided for a widespread psychic need in a simple way.

The father in this philosophy was stripped of his authority and his ability to inspire fear or guilt. The son was self-begotten, innocent, independent of the past. His was his own authority. By constructing "an original relation with the universe," he instituted his own imaginative order, created his own sense of reality, became his own redeemer. He absolved himself of culpability as either a usurping patricide or as a disobedient, defiant, disorderly ingrate desecrating the "sacrifice of the generation of 1776... by.... unwise and unworthy passions." He was no longer doomed to "hurry onward inglorious in ignorance and misery we know not whence, we know not whither" (Rusk, p. 274). The son became a "sufficient substitute" for the whole challenging circumambient world, glorious in his self-knowledge and direction.

For the purposes of this study, the most significant attempt to install a reassuring national authority was expressed as a demand that American literature achieve its cultural independence and interpret experience in the New World. Benjamin T. Spencer notes that American periodicals, especially after 1812, became avowedly nationalistic:

Among the scores of... editorial avowals,... no editor was more uncompromising than John Neal, who, in editing *Brother Jonathan* (1943), cried for "Authors... American to the back bone—American in speech—American in feeling—American through life, and all the changes of life—and American, if it must be so...in death."

A few periodicals, such as the sporting journal *Spirit of the Times* (1847), went so far as to discontinue all British articles in favor of "articles truly American,... presenting the peculiar characteristics of, and illustrating scenes and incidents throughout the Universal Yankee Nation, from the St. Lawrence to the Rio Grande. [Others] content themselves...

with the more flexible aim of reflecting the 'indigenous feelings of our country' and 'the blended radiance of a whole people's mind" (p. 76).

Individual authors were highly self-conscious about the autochthonous flavor of their own and their countrymen's work. Early in his career, Melville voiced his hope for American literature: "This Vermont morning dew is as wet to my feet as Eden's dew to Adam.... We want no American Goldsmiths, no American Miltons.... Let us boldly condemn all imitation" (Lewis, p. 134). In "The American Scholar" **Emerson concluded that American writers had "listed too** long to the courtly muses of Europe," and should attend to the natural music of the new continent.[46] In "Self-Reliance," Emerson assures the cowed American writer that "beauty, convenience, grandeur of thought and quaint expression are as near to us as any; and if the American artist will study with hope and love the precise thing to be done by him, considering the climate, the soil, the length of day, the wants of the people, the habit and form of government, he will create a house in which all these will find themselves fitted, and taste and sentiment will be satisfied also.[47] The "precise thing to be done" by the American artist was to create a constellation of compelling stories that would unify, justify and glorify the nation, however ambiguous and complex its problems, including placating the vengeful Father and alleviating filial remorse and fear. American literature was to structure **experience intelligibly and give the reader a sense of identity** and coherence and direction, a sense of "the end to which God has appointed us." American literature was expected to create an American mythology.

The relationship between literature and myth had been distinctive in America from the beginning. The early settlers came to the New World with old European mythologies derived from the Old World cultures and responsive to Old World social and psychological needs. "Considering the climate, the soil, the length of day, the wants of the people, the habit and form of government," a new house was needed. "Their new circumstances forced new perspectives, new self-concepts, and new world concepts on the colonists and made them see their cultural heritage from angles of vision that non-colonists would find peculiar" (Slotkin, p. 15). These problems of adjustment induced what Philip Wheelwright calls a "mythopoetic mode of consciousness": a readiness to "reason by metaphor... to replace direct statement and logical analysis with figurative or poetic statement" (p. 7).[48]

The urgency of the need to understand and adjust to life "in the wilderness" prompted a proliferation of literary metaphoric models. They came into print quickly, often in the form of narratives of discovery, narratives of Indian war and captivity, sermons and colonization tracts, for several reasons. First, European life in the New World began its development into a distinct culture in the age of the printing press. Secondly, **the highly literate, founding Puritans**

were much inclined toward the writing and printing of books and pamphlets and the creating of elaborate metaphors proving the righteousness of their proceedings. Since Americans turned readily to the printed word for the expression and resolution of doubts, of problems of faith or anxiety and aspiration, literature became the primary vehicle for the communication of mythic material, with the briefest of gaps between the inception of an oral legend and its being fixed in the public print (p. 19).

National mythologies are, of course, normally embodied in a culture's literature, but they usually evolve over centuries of national experience, are transmitted orally, and change according to historical, cultural, psychological and environmental circumstances. In America, such editing, such "natural selection," did not occur. Myths were given formal permanence in literature and became synthetic, literary conventions rather than collective responses generated by the historical experience of the people, and subject to their revision:

Certain instances of experience consistently recurred in each colony; translated into literature, these experiences became stories which recurred in the press with rhythmic persistence. At first such repetition was the result of real recurrence of the experiences. The Indian war and captivity narratives, for example, grew out of the fact that many pious and literary New Englanders were continually falling into the hands of the Indians or attempted to explain their actions in battle. Once in literary form, the experience became available as a vehicle for justifying philosophical and moral values which may have been extrinsic to the initial experience but which preoccupied the minds of the reading public. Thus Cotton Mather and others wrote 'improvements' of the captivity narratives and used them in jeremiads and revival sermons. Through repeated appearances and recastings in the literary marketplace, a narrative which proved viable as a bestseller or a vehicle for religious or commercial persuasions would be imitated by more or less professional writers (where such existed) or those emulous of literary or ecclesiastical reputation. Thus the experience would be reduced to an imitable formula, a literary convention, a romantic version of the myth. When enough literature had been written employing the convention, it might become a sort of given between writer and audience, a set of tacit assumptions on the nature of human experience, on human and divine motivations, on moral values, and on the nature of reality. At this point the convention has some of the force of myth: the experience it portrays has become an image which automatically compels belief by a culture-wide audience in the view of the reality it presents. Thus in tracing the developlment of the conventions of narrative literature, we are tracing the development—by accretion of symbols characteristic of cultural values—of a distinct world vision and an accompanying mythology emerging from the early experiences of Europeans in the wilderness (Slotkin, pp. 20-21).

This relationship between literature and myth in America meant that American myths were peculiarly subject to forces that affect literature. American stories were influenced by current literary fashions; for example, the early nineteenth century's predilection for melodrama was partly responsible for the caricatured representation of the American Indian as a heartless villain or selfless hero. Moroever, when an author aspired to an international reputation, he courted English audiences and observed English conventions that were irrelevant to or destructive of the American effort to understand its situation. Roy Harvey Pearce says that the polarity of characterization of native people in the Indian dramas is due to antithetical English and American literary traditions. Playwrights tried to observe both the conventional English and European melodramatic ennobling of the native American and, at the same time, the American idea of a blood-stained and rude savage. The result of being caught between two traditions, Pearce contends, was that cruelty and barbarism were imputed to Indian characters whose admirable words, actions and ideas were hardly distinguishable from those of the white exemplars.

Another literary factor that worked against more realistic storytelling and thereby against the need to understand the American and his situation, was that many authors had little, if any, first-hand, or even second-hand, experience with American subjects such as the wilderness or the frontier or the Indian, their typical claims of "unimpeachable testimony" **notwithstanding. Instead, they often relied upon highly** literary and artificial sources that were colored by romantic European mythology or by formal conventions of an earlier body of American literature such as the discovery and captivity narratives. Moreover, the authors "usually had ulterior motives in publishing them—a desire to explain or justify, through imaginative reconstruction of events, a course of action they had taken or their right to possess the land, or simply an attempt to persuade potential European settlers of the beauties and wealth of the strange new world" (Pearce, p. 18). "Revival preachers employed Indian war tales as a tool for arousing pious anxiety in their congregations; land speculators used them as advertising ploys; representatives of social, relgious and political factions used them to justify their particular conceptions of the truth" (p. 23). Writing in 1790, John Adams commented on the reliability of accounts of Indian life: "Reasonings from a State of Nature are fallacious, because hypothetical. We have not the facts. Experiments are wanting. Reasonings from Savage Life do not much better. Every writer affirms what he pleases. We have not the facts to be depended on" (p. 253).

The idealism of American mythology and the synthetic production of myths by self-serving literary specialists who had little experience with their subjects, who took their ideas from foreign and domestic literary fashions and conventions, rather than from life, plus the fast pace of the transformation of the fluid myths into fixed literature resulted in a marked discrepancy between American myth and American life. This contributed to uncertainty and despair rather than to the satisfaction and security that national mythologies usually provide.

During the period of this study, such discrepancies became more and more apparent. The myths of America as the hope of the world and authentic Americans as "figures of heroic innocence and vast potentialities" (Lewis, p. 1), laboring in the Vineyards of the Lord, were suspect. The myth of God and human nature and republicanism as allies was widely discredited by American experience. The result was a call for the printed word to clarify and soothe, a call for a new, independent American literature "to communicate the novelty of experience in the New World" as *The Democratic Review* put it in an editorial in its November issue of 1839. An American Homer or an American Shakespeare was expected immediately, an expectation probably influenced by the earlier pace of the transformation of myth into literature. Critics thought that an American epic, perhaps the most obvious myth-like literary form (as I have defined cultural myth), was just around the corner.

The nature of "the novelty of experience in the New World" gave rise to much debate in periodicals, such as *The North American Review, The Atlantic Magazine, The Southern Review* and *The Port Folio*, as well as in addresses and orations on all sorts of occasions. A common question was what were the distinctive materials for a geniuine American literature[50] that would satisfy the prevailing romantic literary preferences **for splendid and sentimental effects, spectacular, strange and** thrilling scenes, inspirational themes and simple, melodramatic plots? Many despaired of finding any peculiarly American literary materials. The most extreme thought that there was something about America that blighted the poetic imagination. "What effort of genius," one exclaimed, "can breathe the least spirit of poetry or romance into the cold, calculating prudence of American life?"[51]

American history seemed too recent,[52] too ignobly familiar, too likely to divide rather than unify. Walter Channing, the Unitarian minister, complained that "we lack a remote antiquity."[53] It lacked romance:

Our history is allied to the calmness and plainness of intellect rather than to the hurry and splendor of the imagination; it is distinguished rather for an inflexible adherence to principles, than for a vast variety of brilliant achievements. The spirit in which our fathers opposed the last hazards, resembles the stern intrepidity of Romulus, or the tranquil resolution of Socrates, not the effervesence of a passionate young hero on a field of glory.[54]

The present seemed equally unromantic. The critic who reviewed James Kirke Paulding's *Backwoodsman* in *The Port Folio* noted:

We have no ferocious giants, no frowning battlements, no lordly knights or distressed damsels. With us, all is plain, simple, unsophisticated nature. The most terrible necromancer among us is the sheriff, whose gates readily open on the exhibition of a piece of paper. In such utter absence of anything like a hero or even a suitable scene for a poet's eye in fine frenzy to roll upon, it required uncommon nerves and powerful motives to publish an epic lay.[55]

No poet's eye could roll in fine frenzy upon prosaic, unstratified American society, either. Cooper, for example, who was not yet in 1828 quarreling with his countrymen, wrote:

I very well know there are theorists that assume that the society and institutions of this country are, or ought to be, particularly favorable to novelties and variety. But the experience of one month, in these states, is sufficient to show any man the falsity of their position. The effect of a promiscuous assemblage anywhere is to create a standard of deportment; and great liberty permits everyone to aim at its attainment. I have never seen a nation so much alike in my life, as the people of the United States, and what is more, they are not only like each other, but they are remarkably like that which common sense tells them they ought to resemble. No doubt traits of character that are a little peculiar, without, however, being very poetical, or very rich, are to be found in remote districts; but they are rare and not always happy exceptions. In short, it is not possible to conceive a state of society, in which more of the attributes of plain good sense, or fewer of the artificial absurdities of life, are to be found, than here. There is no costume for the peasant, (there is scarcely a peasant at all), no wig for the judge, no baton for the general, no diadem for the chief magistrate. The darkest ages of their history are illuminated by the light of truth. The utmost efforts of their chivalry are limited by the laws of God; and even the deeds of their sages and heroes are to be sung **in a language that would differ but little from a version of the ten** commandments. However useful and respectable this may be in actual life, it indicates but one direction to the man of genius.[56]

John Bristed, a well known writer of the second quarter of the nineteenth century, complained that democratic institutions reduced the citizenry to a homogeneity and were responsible for the lack of good novels. "Of native novels we have no great stock, and none good," he said, and continued, explaining:

Our democratic institutions placing all the people on a dead level of political equality; and the pretty equal diffusion of property throughout the country affords but little room for varieties and contrasts of character; nor is there much scope for fiction, as the country is quite new, and all that has happened from its first settlement to the present hour, respecting it, is known to everyone. There is, to be sure, some traditionary romance about the Indians; but a novel describing these miserable barbarians, their squaws, and papooses, would not be very interesting to the present race of American readers.[57]

The American environment, however, was both interesting and distinctive. The poet James Hillhouse, who found American history uninspiring, wrote glowingly of the American wilderness:

True we have no mouldering ruins of feudal power, and none of the romantic legends which linger round them, to elicit the unsuspected spark of genius, and to fan its flame. Our forests breathe upon us the freshness of primeval nature.... Whoever rises here, must rise by irrepressible internal energies, and the impulse of noblest inspirations—the grand eternal forms of nature. Vast, solitary and sublime, pressing on the mind the symbols of creative power, rather than mementoes of departed human pride, our scenery carries the thoughts more immediately up to those ultimate conceptions which should be bound, like the holy gems of divination on the breast of a superior genius. It may stamp our poetry with the image of its own virgin grandeur; its influence confirmed by the want of a national heroic or barbarous age, may direct us toward the springs of our religion; which, whenever smitten by a commissioned rod, will gush forth purer and more abundant waters than ever flowed from Hippocrine (Hillhouse, pp. 31-32).

In reviewing the poem "Gertrude of Wyoming" by Thomas Campbell, in which the Indian chief is characteristically described as "the man without a tear," Washington Irving predicted that the poem might "assist to convince many, who were before slow to believe that our country is capable of inspiring the highest poetic feelings, though destitute of the hackneyed materials of poetry." In America, he says, there are no nightingales, no dryads, no satyrs, but "wherever nature displays herself in simple beauty of wild magnificence or wherever the human mind appears in new and striking situations, neither the poet nor the philosopher can want subjects worthy of his genius."[58]

Nature in America had long been perceived as distinctive. Philip Freneau had referred to the Mississippi as "this prince of rivers in comparison with which the Nile is but a small rivulet, and the Danube is a ditch."[59] Abigail Adams observed that European birds did not sing as melodiously as American birds[60] and other travelers judged the Adirondacks superior to the Alps (Nash, p. 83). Such, of course, had no basis in fact. The Danube was not a ditch, European birds sang as melodiously; the Alps were not inferior. Nationalistic literature would have to focus elsewhere.

Nature was not enough; an attribute unique to nature in the New World had to be found. The search led to the wilderness. In the early nineteenth century American nationalists began to understand that it was in the wilderness of its nature that their country was unmatched. While other nations might have an occasional wild peak or patch of woods, there was no equivalent to a wild continent (Nash, p. 69).

The deists, moreover, had popularized the belief that the "Divine Author" of the universe had impressed Himself most clearly in the wilderness, and that there man might "feel... his soul expand under the mighty influence of nature in her primitive beauty and strength."[61] "There is no religion in it," declared Estwick Evans,[62] a New Hampshire lawyer who walked four thousand miles to the West with his two dogs.

There was beauty too.

Sublimity gained widespread usage in the eighteenth century. As an aesthetic category the sublime dispelled the notion that beauty in nature was seen only in the comfortable, fruitful, and well-ordered. Vast, chaotic scenery could also please.... Such ideas greatly broadened the classical conception of ordered, proportioned beauty (Nash, pp. 46-47).

Novelists such as James Fenimore Cooper, Robert Montgomery Bird, Charles Webber and William Gilmore Simms made use of the wilderness and its inhabitants.[63] After his early English imitation, *Precaution* (1820), Cooper became, for a while, a national literary hero not only because of his penetration into the fundamental American myth of an innocent relationship between two men of different races who forsake all others and flee from civilization to a fresh world, but also because he realized the literary possibilities of the wilderness in his Leatherstocking stories. Natty Bumppo expresses all the romantic conventions about wilderness: its sanctity, its beauty, its beneficence. He feels "the holy calm of nature,"[64] and describes Nature as his sweetheart: "She's in the forest... hanging from the boughs of the trees, in a soft rain—in the dew on the open grass—the clouds that float about in the blue heavens—the birds that sing in the woods... and in all the other glorious gifts that come from God's Providence" (p. 129). William Cullen Bryant celebrated the American wilds for themselves and as "God's first temples" ("A Forest Hymn"). The action of the Indian dramas is laid in dark gorges and deep forests and on precipitous cliffs, "where man, erect, can walk a manly round" (Barker, p. 580).

Although the wilderness was readily accepted as material for a distinctive American literature, its inhabitant, the Indian, was not. "A novel describing these miserable barbarians, their squaws and papooses could not be interesting to the present race of American readers" (p. 356), charged John Bristed. James Hillhouse allowed that although Indian history alone could provide instances of "outraged affection, remorseless cruelty, or dire revenge," nonetheless the savage character "possesses too little variety for extended effects" (p. 30). "Of the mummery of aboriginal superstition little can be learned, and of that little... nothing can be made," remarked a writer for *The Atlantic Magazine* in 1824. The *United States Literary Gazette* found the Indian utterly unsuitable:

We hear much of the innocence, pure nature, and enchanting oratory of the savage, and the conclusion has been drawn, that poetry declines as civilization advances. But no one has examined Indian eloquence, without knowing, that it is confined within a very limited range.... He can apostrophize sensible objects in impetuous language. But his life is spent in hunting, sleeping and unnatural crime. From the very nature of the case he is an utter stranger to a great variety of feelings known to a civilized community.[65]

A few defended the Indian as a suitable subject "worthy of American genius," a subject for autochtonous American romantic fiction, folktale and even epic poetry. Caroline Kirkland, a frontier writer of the 1830s and 40s, argued along with Eastern writers like Longfellow, that the Indians were the "only distinct and characteristic poetic material to which we, as Americans, have an unqualified right" (Spencer, p. 104). Washington Irving agreed. A reviewer of *The Last of the Mohicans* saw them as more than "fit":

The aborigines of our soil constitute the great machinery of the piece.... We have long since looked upon the character of the North American savage as one admirably calculated to form an engine of great power in the hands of some ingenious master of romance... and the success with which it has been managed by Mr. Cooper in the present work is a striking example of its effect.[66]

(The reviewer also noted that "the Indians are admirable instruments of romance, but our author works them to death," p. 166.) Instead of little being known about "the mummery of aboriginal superstition," another writer pointed out that "one may learn as much as one wants, by reading the accounts of those who have examined the subject; and he may make as much use as he is able."[67] Variety was required, and the customs, ceremonies, "fabulous legends and religious superstitions" of the Indian could provide it.

If scenes of unparalleled torture and indefatigable endurance, persevering vengeance, and unfailing friendship, hair-breadth escapes, and sudden ambush; if horrors of gloomy forests and unexplored caverns, tenanted by the most horrible of banditti; if faith in wild predictions, and entire submission of the soul to power of ancient legends and visionary prophecies, are useful to the poet or romancer, here they may be found in abundance and endless variety (Sedgwick, p. 150).

The writer goes on to say that poetry is inherent in "the conceptions and notions of some of our aborigines." He observes that their mythology is more refined and less ridiculous than the Hindus.

In worshipping the Great Spirit, the American Indian may be regarded as worshipping the creative intellect and invoking the faculty of pure imagination. Prophecy, which the Indian identifies with poetry, could serve the epic's turn; [moreover,] he who would use this machinery in verse would not need to introduce barbarous names, unsusceptible of being euphemized; but may employ, directly, the personification of the Deity and its attributes; and in so doing, speak the universally intelligible language of society (Sedgwick, p. 150).

William Tudor, founder and first editor of *The North American Review*, enthusiastically compared Indian character, life and history to those of the Greek heroic age.[68]

These Indians perhaps exhibited the counterpart of what the Greeks were in the heroic ages and particularly the Spartans during the vigor of their institutions.... These episodes [Ulysses and Diomed and Nesus and Euryolus] are two of the finest in those immortal epics, yet it is only to the genius of Homer and Virgil that they are indebted for more than may be found in several Indian adventures.[69]

Tudor did not find their oratory "confined within a very limited range" and praised their dignified speeches and "solemnity of their councils" as being consistent with epic character.

The speeches ascribed by Homer to the heroes of the *Iliad and Odyssey* form some of the finest passages in these poems.... The speeches of these Indians only want similar embellishments to excite admiration.... Perilous and romantic adventures, figurative and eloquent harangues, strong contrasts and important interests are as frequent in this portion of history as the theatre on which these actions were performed is abundant in grand and beautiful scenery (Sedgwick, p. 149).

In the South, William Gilmore Simms, anticipating the Indian Dramas, proclaimed the Indians to be Greek-tragic victims, "whose melancholy history would afford a high theme for an American drama" (Spencer, p. 105).

Civilized life in America might be as dull as "broad and simple daylight," but the life of the Indian was as exciting and mysterious as the pathless wilds. The texture of American society might be thin: here was a thickening agent. America might not have any peasants, nor any ferocious giants, nor any aristocracy or clergy, but there were Indians, "our aborigines," and authenticity clung "even to their corpses." America might want for European antiquity, but it did not want for an ancient history "with coppery tints and reflections," as Thoreau said. It might lack a mythology, but the Indian had a refined mythology "less ridiculous than the Hindus" (Sedgwick, p. 150). Here was the sublime, the wonderful, the picturesque, and the pathetic that popular task demanded and explicitly received in the Indian dramas.

As we have seen, Indians were "engine[s] of great power" in other capacities. They were "great machinery" for self-definition through repudiation: "The idea of savagism became a way to make men know the triumph, the pain, and the final glory in being a civilized American" (Pearce, p. 212). Slotkin has shown that American identity was created not only through repudiation but also through affirmation of Indian cultures. The native American myth of the hunter/warrior who incorporates the properties of the consumed prey was adopted by whites to explain American identity and destiny. This myth of regeneration through violence is clearly expressed in the seminal *Daniel Boone* by John Filson. The hunter/hero forges a distinctive American character through repeated immersions in the wilderness. During these episodes he becomes like the Indian he hunts and thereby achieves a higher state of being (Slotkin, pp. 268-313). In the Indian Dramas this myth informs the characterization of the Indian-like American hero as the untutored, courageous, stoic, self-possessed republican who loves the solitude and freedom of the wild land and who lives by the violence of Indian warfare.

Robert Berkhofer argues that despite identification through the Indian, whites justified Indian policies by perceiving and evaluating the Indian as utterly and irremediably other (Berkhofer, p. xvi). During the Jacksonian era Indians were perceived as threatened with extinction because of differences[70] that were inherent and immutable because of Indian arrestment in the childhood of social development. This became a rationalization for dispossession and justified Jackson's removal policies. It satisfied both those who feared Indian extinction as well as those who wanted further Indian land cessions.

According to Rogin, the myths and images of Indians as children was important to the psychological development of whites. He argues that the "Indian policy of death and dispossession [which] is justified by the paternal benevolence of a father for his children" enabled Americans to achieve a flawed maturity, unavailable through mature sexual pleasure because of the whites' limited libidinal force. He further contends that American culture "undermined the authority provided by history, tradition, family connections, and the other ties of old European existence" (p. 9), which created a need to legitimate authority, whether it was political or familial. This need was fulfilled by an ostensible paternalism toward Indians, a policy consistently maintained by Andrew Jackson, "whose life was a symbol for his age" (pp. 10-14).

The preoccupation with the politics of parent/child relationships and with "red children" in the Indian Dramas reflects these needs for identification, authority and exoneration. The myths of these plays absolve Americans of patricidal guilt by discrediting and denying fathers, and at the same time relieve filial anxiety by sanctioning ancestral authority through the apotheosis of authority figures and through submission to the will of God the Father. American claims to authoritative maturity are justified by paternalism toward the Indian.

The guilt emanating from Indian policy is also absolved by **dehumanizing and vilifying the Indian, and justifying** aggressive expansionism as the will of the "inscrutable Arbiter" (Brown, p. 189). Whites are characterized as divinely appointed Lords of Creation come to "sowe spirituals and reape temporals" (Purchas, p. 7), thereby "hewing a road" (Custis, p. 194) to "Glory's farthest goal" (Owen, p. 153), leaving in their path Indian corpses carved with crosses. The Indian had proven "tolerable and fit to be made use of."

Thus the Indian Dramas along with ancestor worship, the revival of religious and moral fervor, and the philosophy of

"The Imperial Self," soothed the American psyche, appeasing the ghosts of the Indian and the father. They provided a comforting and credible vision of national realities which satisfied psychological needs in terms of American historical experience and environment. They were a part of the anxious quest for the pillar of fire to follow.

Notes

Chapter 1

[1]My discussion of myths and mythogenesis is based on the following works: Joseph Campbell, *Myths to Live By*; Michael Novak, *The Experience of the Nothingness*; Richard Slotkin, *Regeneration Through Violence: The Mythology of the American Frontier, 1600-1860*.

[2]Frank Waters, *The Man Who Killed the Deer* (Flagstaff, Arizona: Northland Press, 1942), pp. 28-29.

[3]Richard Slotkin, *Regeneration Through Violence: The Mythology of The American Frontier, 1600-1860* (Middletown, Conn.: Wesleyan Univ. Press, 1973), p. 7.

[4]Michael Novak, *The Experience of Nothingness* (New York: Harper and Row, 1970), p. 17.

[5]Eric Heller, *The Works of Nietzsche,* Tape Casette Curriculum, Everett Edwards, Inc.

[6]Joseph Campbell, *Myths to Live By* (New York: Viking Press, 1972), p. 11.

[7]Thomas Merton, *Conjectures of a Guilty Bystander* (New York: Doubleday, 1965), pp. 23-29.

[8]Frances Jennings, *The Invasion of Ameica: Indians, Colonialism, and the Cant of Conquest* (Chapel Hill, N.C.: Univ. of North Carolina Press, 1975), p. 15.

[9]Perry Miller, *Errand into the Wilderness* (Cambridge, Mass.: Harvard Univ. Press, 1956).

[10]Quoted in Angie Debo, *A History of the Indians of the United States* (Norman: Univ. of Oklahoma Press, 1970), p. 48.

[11]Roy Harvey Pearce, *The Savages of America: A Study of the Indian and the Idea of Civilizaton* (Baltimore: Johns Hopkins Press, 1965), pp. 19-23.

[12]Robert F. Berkhofer, Jr., *The White Man's Indian: Images of the American Indian from Columbus to the Present* (New York: Knopf, 1978), p. 80.

[13]Maude Bodkin, *Archetypal Patterns in Poetry* (London: Oxford Univ. Press, 1963), p. 2.

[14]Robert Dale Owen, Preface to *Pocahontas* (New York: George Dearborn Publisher, 1837), p. 1.

[15]R.W.B. Lewis, *The American Adam: Innocence, Tragedy, and Tradition in the Nineteenth Century* (Chicago: Univ. of Chicago Press, 1964), p. 5.

[16]Quoted in Russel B. Nye, *The Almost Chosen People: Essays in the History of American Ideas* (East Lansing: Michigan State Univ. Press, 1966), p. 173.

[17]Paul C. Nagel, *This Sacred Trust: American Nationality, 1789-1898* (New York: Oxford Univ. Press, 1971), p. 115.

[18]Arthur Hobson Quinn, *A History of the American Drama* (New York: F.S. Crofts, 1943), p. 275.

[19]Albert Keiser, *The Indian in American Literature* (New York: Oxford Univ. Press, 1933), p. 95.

²⁰Montrose Moses, *The American Dramatist* (Boston: Little, Brown & Co., 1911), p. 95.

²¹An ostensible exception appears in the chapter on Cooper. Keiser denies General Lewis Cass' charge that Cooper idealized and romanticized the Indian. He asserts that the majority of Cooper's Indians are unlike the heroic Chingackook and Uncas. Keiser regards Magua as the typical Cooper Indian.

Chapter 2

¹Henry Brackenridge, *1782 Letter on Indian Atrocities: Narratives of the Perils and the Suffering of Dr. Knight and John Slover Among the Indians During the Revolutionary War* (Cincinnati, Oh.: N.P., 1867), p. 62.

²General Philip Henry Sheridan. Quoted in Edward S. Ellis *The History of Our Country* (Indianapolis, Ind.: N.P., 1900), p. 1483.

³Charlotte Barnes, *The Forest Princess or Two Centuries Ago* from *Play, Prose, and Poetry,* by Charlotte M.S. Barnes (Philadelphia: E.H. Butler & Co., 1848), p. 1.

⁴The general historical unreliability of these plays is illustrated by the suspect character of the "unimpeachable source" cited by the author of one of four plays about Pocahontas. For "The Forest Princess," Barnes used Captain John Smith's self-advertising *The Generall Historie of Virginia, New England, and The Summer Isles* (1624). Albert Keiser judges Smith's account to be highly exaggerated or even utterly imaginative, designed to satisfy the adventurer's love of the marvel ʾs and aggrandizing (Keiser, pp. 2-6). Smith's exaggeration has been documented more recently by Philip L. Barbour in *The Three Worlds of John Smith* (Boston: Houghton Mifflin, 1964).

⁵Henry Thoreau assembled eleven notebooks of material about native peoples, including Eskimos and Latin Americans, over approximately the last twelve years of his life, which he probably intended to use in an Indian history of the United States. The unpublished and generally unknown notebooks are the property of the Pierpont Morgan Library.

⁶Henry R. Dobyns, "Estimating Aboriginal American Population: An Appraisal of Techniques with a New Hemispheric Estimate," *Current Anthropology,* Oct. 1966, Vol. 7, No. 4, pp. 395-416. Francis Jennings argues that scholars' estimates of the size of the aboriginal populations are affected by their concept of savagery: "Proponents of the concept of savagery stipulate, among other things, that large populations are impossible in savage societies. It follows that if aboriginal populations can be shown to have been large, they could not have been savage." He regards Dobyns' calculations as "conservative and meticulously reasoned." Francis Jennings, *The Invasion of America: Indians, Colonials, and the Cant of Conquest* (Chapel Hill, N.C.: Institute of Early American History and Culture by the University of North Carolina Press, 1975), p. 30.

⁷The following discussion of the similarities of American Indian cultures relies heavily on the following works: John Collier, *Indians of the Americas: The Long Hope*; Francis Jennings, *The Invasion of America: Indians, Colonialism and the Cant of Conquest*; Wilcomb E. Washburn, *The Indian in America.*

⁸Frederick Turner III and Virginia Armstrong, ed., *I Have Spoken* (Chicago: Swallow Press, 1971), p. xi.

⁹Speech of Chief Seattle, *The Washington Historical Quarterly,* 22, No. 4 (Oct. 1931), The Washington University State Historical Society, Seattle, Washington.

¹⁰Helen Addison Howard, *War Chief Joseph* (Caldwell, Ind.: The Caxton Printers, Ltd., 1941), p. 84.

¹¹Chief Luther Standing Bear, *Land of the Spotted Eagle* (Boston: Houghton Mifflin, 1911, p. 163.

¹²Washburn (p. 48) notes that this unanimity principle was often more apparent than real because the dissenting individual would withdraw rather than confront the opposition.

[13]Social control was not unknown and ranged from humor and ridicule to whipping and death, although the latter was uncommon (Washburn, pp. 40-42). Washburn notes, however, that Native American child-rearing practices rarely included corporal punishment.

[14]Based on the research of Laura Thompson (*Personality and Government: Findings and Recommendations of the Indian Administration Research* [Mexico City, 1951] into child-rearing practices among Native Americans, Washburn concludes that these practices "discouraged competitive, egocentric, and defensive attitudes... and encouraged cooperative, self-confident, and secure behavior" (p. 14).

[15]This is not to deny the existence of envy and greed. Moreover the giver expected the generosity to be repaid in time of need (Washburn, p. 21).

[16]Bruce Trigger notes that European philosophers and social critics such as Montaigne often used the noble savage myth as a polemical device to criticize their own societies (*Ethnohistory*, xxii [1975], pp. 51-56).

[17]Harold E. Fey and D'Arcy McNickle, *Indians and Other Americans: Two Ways of Life Meet* (New York: Harper & Row, 1970), p. 22.

[18]John Heckewelder, *Account of the History, Manners, and Customs of the Indian Nations, Who Once Inhabited Pennsylvania and the Neighboring States* (Philadelphia: American Philosophical Society, 1819), pp. 85-86.

[19]Perry Miller, *Writings of Roger Williams*, VII (New York: Russell & Russell, 1963), p. 4.

[20]Cited in Dee Brown, *Bury My Heart at Wounded Knee* (New York: Holt, Rinehart & Winston, 1970), p. 316.

[21]William Brandon, *The American Heritage Book of Indians* (New York: American Heritage Publishing Co., 1961), p. 244.

[22]Americans, along with other agrarian idealists, believed in the natural and divine superiority of farming to hunting. Pearce notes that the origins of this belief are economic, biblical, Lockean and scientific. "For Locke—and virtually all Americans were, in the most general sense, Lockeans—man achieved his highest humanity by taking something out of nature and converting it with his labor into part of himself. His private property conceived of in terms of the close, personal relationship of an agrarian society, was his means to social maturity. It gave him stability, self-respect, privacy and the basis for civilized society. For Americans, the Lockean theory must have made savage society seem loose, immature, virtually anarchic, full of the false freedom of doing what one pleases..." (Pearce, p 68). Scientist Arnold Buyot, lecturing at Harvard in 1849, said that, in order for the "vegetative, insensitive, and cold" Indian to become civilized, he must not "surrender to nature" but "exploit her" as God had intended.

[23]There was a continuing effort in the eighteenth century, with some notable successes, such as those of the great awakening in the 1740s in the English colonies; nonetheless, the hope for widespread acceptance of the "good news" had dimmed (Washburn, p. 114). Berkhofer notes that seventeenth- and early eighteenth-century experience had led whites, laymen and missionaries alike, to the conclusion that "Reds and whites were inherently incompatible" (p. 79).

[24]George Catlin, the celebrated American artist who traveled and painted in the West during the 1830s, wrote of the Indians: "I love a people who have always made me welcome to the best they had... who are honest without laws, who have no jails and no poor-houses... who never take the name of God in vain... who worship God without a Bible, and I believe God loves them also... who are free from religious animosities... who have never raised a hand against me, or stolen my property, where there is no law to punish either... who never fought a battle with white men except on their own ground... and Oh, how I love a people who don't live for the love of money!" George Catlin, Letter from St. Louis, in Thomas Donaldson, "The George Catlin Indian Gallery," Smithsonian Institution, *Annual Report*, V, p. 505.

[25]J.B. Tyrell, ed., *David Thompson's Narrative of His Explorations in Western America, 1784-1812* (Toronto, Can.: The Champlain Society, 1961), p. 11.

[26]John Collier, *Indians of the Americas: The Long Hope* (New York: The New American Library, 1947), p. 142.

[27]Wilcomb E. Washburn, ed., *The Indian and the White Man* (Garden City, N.Y.: Doubleday, 1964), pp. 209-214.

[28]Hazel W. Hertzberg, *The Search for an American Indian Identity: Modern Pan-Indian Movements* (Syracuse,N.Y., 1971), p. 1.

[29]Thomas Franham, "Travels in the Great Western Prairies (1843)" in Thwaites, ed., *Early Western Travels*, MMVIII, pp. 123-124. Quoted in Pearce, p. 64.

[30]Chief Seattle of the Dwamish, spoken to Isaac Stevens, Governor of Washington Territory in 1854, quoted in *I Have Spoken*, Virginia Armstrong, ed. (Chicago: Sage Books, 1971), pp. 77-79.

[31]James Elliot Cabot, *A Memoir of Ralph Waldo Emerson*, II (Cambridge: Riverside Press, 1887), pp. 697-702.

[32]In a psychoanalytic analysis of Jackson, Michael Paul Rogin contends that Jackson, "the single figure most responsible for Indian destruction in pre-Civil War America," was monomaniacal about eliminating Indians because he had projected his disturbed inner world onto the outer world. As a result Indian wars, Indian treaties, and Indian removal became the media through which Jackson achieved a "contaminated" maturity expressed as paternal authority (pp. 13-15).

[33]The idea of an exchange of eastern Indian lands for lands west of the Mississippi originated with Thomas Jefferson, and the policy of permanent removal was developed during Monroe's administration (Berkhofer, p. 137).

Chapter 3

[1]Letter from Columbus to Luis Santangel in Julius E. Olson and Edward Gaylord Bourne, eds., "The Northmen, Columbus, and Cabot, 985-1501," in *Early Narratives of American History Series* (New York: Scribner's, 1906), pp. 73-74. Quoted in Forbes, p. 9.

[2]Jane Cecil, trans., *The Journal of Christopher Columbus* (New York: Clarkson N. Potter, 1960), pp. 23-24.

[3]Gary B. Nash, "The Image of the Indian in the Southern Colonial Mind," *William and Mary Quarterly*, April 1972, Vol. 29, No. 2, pp. 197-230.

[4]Arthur Roy Buntin,"The Indian in American Literature, 1680-1760" (Dissertation, Univ. of Washington, 1961), p. 120.

[5]William Hubbard, *A Narrative of the Troubles with the Indians in New England* (Boston), 1:24. Quoted in Samuel G. Drake, *The History of the Indian Wars in New England* (New York: B. Franklin, 1971), pp. 52-53.

[6]Richard Van Der Beets, ed., *Held Captive by Indians: Selected Narratives, 1642-1836* (Knoxville: Univ. of Tennessee Press, 1973), p. 77.

[7]Carl Van Doren, ed., *Benjamin Franklin's Autobiographical Writings* (New York: Viking, 1945), p. 724.

[8]Hawthorne's short story "Maypole at Merrymount" is based on Morton's effort to reinstitute the May games, which the Puritans regarded as a pagan rout, among the Indians.

[9]Thomas Morton, *New English Canaan: Containing an Abstract of New England Composed in Three Books; the First Setting Forth the Originall of the Natives, Their Manners and Customs; Together with their tractable Nature and Love Towards the English; II. The Natural Endowments of the Countrie, and what Staple Commodities it Yieldeth; III. What People are Planted There, Their Prosperity, What Remarkable Accidents Have Happened Since Their First Planting of it; together with Their Tenets and Practice of Their Church; in Peter Force, ed., Forces Tracts and Other Papers Relating Principally to the Origin, Settlement and Progress of the Colonies in North America, from the Discovery of the Country to the Year 1776*. 2 No. 5 (1838).

[10]William Smith and Thomas Hutchinson, *Historical Account of the Expedition Against the Ohio Indians, in the year 1764, Under the Command of Henry Boquet, Esq., Colonel of the Foot, and New Brigadier General in America: Including his Transactions with the Indians, Relative to the Delivery of Their Prisoners, and the Preliminaries of Peace; With an Introductory Account of the Preceding Campaign, and Battle at Bushy-Run; to which are Annexed Military Papers, Containing Reflections on the War with the Savages* (Philadelphia: William Bradford, 1765), Cited in Slotkin, pp. 231-235.

[11]In 1802 Joseph Croswell had published a New Englandized Pocahontas story in blank verse, titled: "A New World Planted or The Adventures of the Forefathers of New England, who Landed in Plymouth, December 22, 1620." It was the love story of Pocahontas, daughter of King Massasoit, and the English settler, Hampden. They prove that red and white "gifts" (Cooper's word) do mix, provided the red is royal, beautiful, intelligent and exemplary.

[12]Fiedler suggests that this representation partially accounts for Cooper's popularity. It accommodated both the general ambivalence toward the Indian and the bifurcated points of view. See *Love and Death in the American Novel* (New York: Criterion Books, 1960), pp. 193-194.

[13]The following plays are listed by Keiser, p. 65, as either imperfectly recorded or entirely vanished: "The Manhattoes"; "Narramattah"; "The Maid of Wyoming"; "The Wigwam"; "The Indian Wife"; "The Last of the Mohicans"; "Miantanimoh"; "The Liberty Tree"; "Lamorah"; "Wacousta"; "The Pioneers"; "Oronaska or the Chief of the Mohawks"; "Kairrissah"; "Outallissi"; "The Yemassee"; "Sassacus"; "Tippecanoe"; "Sharratah"; "Osceola"; "Telula, of the Star of Hope"; "Onoleetah"; "The Eagle Eye"; "Couista, or the Lion of the Forest"; "The Star of the West"; "Onylda, or the Pequot Maid"; "Oroonoka"; "The Silver Knife, or the Hunters of the Rocky Mountains"; "Tuscatomba"; "Tutoona"; "Wissahickon"; "Mioutouman." Keiser, Pearce and Quinn agree that there were approximately thirty-five Indian plays in twenty years and that about eighteen are extant. Walter Meserve in *An Outline History of American Drama* (Totowa, New Jersey: Littlefield, Adams & Co., 1965), p. 76, estimates that fifty Indian dramas were performed between 1825 and 1860.

[14]Plays with dual titles will be referred to by only the first hereafter.

[15]Arthur Hobson Quinn, *A History of American Drama* (New York: Harper & Bros., 1923), p. 270.

[16]Many of these plays were never published because there was no copyright protection. Where publishing information exists, it will be included in the documentation.

[17]The only other extant plays I find reference to are "The Indian Prophecy" (1827) by G.W.P. Custis; "Desoto, The Hero of the Mississippi" (1852) by G.H. Miles; and "William Penn or The Elm Tree" (1829) by R.P. Smith. The one copy of the last is in the Historical Society of Pennsylvania in Philadelphia. The location of the others is unknown.

Indian material was so insistently demanded that Indian fiction proliferated, predominantly as sentimental and noisomely bloodcurdling novels, which evolved into the dime novel after 1850. Some of the most noteworthy were: *Hobomok* (1824) by Lydia Marie Child; *Hope Leslie* (1827) by Catherine Marie Sedgwick; *The Shoshone Valley* (1830) by Timothy Flint; *The Yemassee* (1835) by William Gilmore Simms; *Legends of the West* (1832) by James Hall; *Old Hicks, The Guide* (1848) by Charles Webber; *Nick of the Woods* (1837) by Robert Montgomery Bird; *Tales of the Northwest* (1830) by William Joseph Snelling.

[18]Robert Berkhofer notes the persistence and perpetuation of the dual image of noble savage and savage savage without substantial modification or variation over four centuries of American history. He attributes this, in part, to the white tendency to understand the Indian as the antithesis of themselves. Since whites were consistently dynamic and historical, the Indian must be static and ahistorical to remain Indian: he must not change (p. 29). This affected the primogeniture case for land claims: if there was no past, no history, there were no primogeniture rights.

[19]J.N. Barker, *The Indian Princess or La Belle Sauvage* (Philadelphia: T. & G. Palmer, Printers, 1808) in Montrose Moses, *Representative Plays by American Dramatists* (New York: Benjamin Blom, Inc., 1948), p. 610.

[20]General Alexander Macomb, *Pontiac or The Siege of Detroit: A Drama in Three Acts* (Boston: S. Colman, Printer, 1835), p. 49.

[21]John A. Stone, *Metamora or The Last of the Wampanoags* (New York, 1829). Included in Ralph H. Ware and H.W. Schoenberger, *America's Lost Plays*, Vol. 13-14 (Bloomington: Indiana Univ. Press, 1940), p. 37.

[22]William Emmons, *Tecumseh or The Battle of the Thames* (Philadelphia: N.P., 1836), p. 14.

[23]Nathanial Deering, *Carabasset: A Tragedy in Five Acts* (Portland, ME.: S. Colman, Printer, 1830), p. 23.

[24]George Washington Parke Custis, *Pocahontas or The Settlers of Virginia* (Philadelphia, 1827) in A.H. Quinn, *Representative American Plays* (New York: Century, 1917), p. 198.

[25]This play was dedicated to Governor Lewis Cass of the Michigan Territory, who voiced the first serious criticism of Cooper's Indians. In the *North American Review* of January 1826, he applied his standards of Indian naturalism to *The Last of the Mohegans* and concluded that "the last of the Mohegans is an Indian of the school of Mr. Heckewelder, a Moravian missionary to the Delawares, and not of the school of nature." Of other Cooper Indians, Cass declared that they "have no living prototype in our forests." James Grossman, *James Fenimore Cooper* (New York: W. Sloan, 1949), pp. 47-48.

[26]**Lewis Deffebach, *Oolaita, An Indian Heroine* (Philadelphia: N.P., 1821).**

[27]Joseph Doddridge, *Logan, the Last of the Race of Skikellemus, Chief of the Cayuga Nation* (Buffalo Creeks, VA.: N.P., 1823), performed 1821.

[28]George Jones, *Tecumseh and the Prophet of the West, an Original Historical Israel-Indian Tragedy* (New York: Harper & Bros., 1844), p. 15.

[29]**Barker's Pocahontas speaks like Shakespeare's Juliet:**"And 'tis the screaming bird of night I hear, / not the melodious mocking bird," p. 612.

[30]In other words, she is given the training of a European lady, despite Rolfe's earlier assertion that "Rather than wed a European dame, I'd take a squaw of the woods and get papooses" (p. 581). He seems to get both.

[31]In *The Octoroon*, the "divers colour'd fruit" awaiting the All-American plucker is black—or has one drop of black blood out of every eight of red American drops. These drops "burn in her veins and light up her heart like a foggy sun" (p. 9), according to one of the many white men who are in love with her, yet she acts like one of Hawthorne's palefaced virgins. Dion Boucicault, *The Octoroon or Life in Louisiana* (New York: S. French & Son, 1859).

[32]The only Indian matron herein is Mantea, the mother of the children of the English settler Barclay. She is merely an instrument of the plot, but she shares the qualities of unquestioning loyalty and subservience with the other matrons in the Pocahontas plays.

[33]Owen, p. 149. A nineteenth-century art critic who saw a portrait of Pocahontas described her as "an intellectual beauty." See Keiser, p. 18.

[34]Melinda does acknowledge, however, that "the woman of our blood doth know her place" (p. 69), by which she means subordinate to men, not in the front lines of battle.

[35]Jones, p. 14. Tecumseh has a pathological veneration for the Mother. He speaks of his mother's "sacred hands" (p. 72) and "spher'd shrines" (p. 39). Her heart is "pure nature's home" (p. 39) and the "altar of the world" (p. 39).

[36]Pocahontas is often referred to as "The Nonpareil of Virginia."

[37]In his *Sketch Book*, Washington Irving described King Philip (Metamora) as an amiable and lofty character, with "feelings of connubial love and paternal tenderness, and with generous sentiments of friendship, proudness of heart, and an untamable love of natural liberty." Washington Irving, *Sketch Book* (Philadelphia: Lea & Blanchard, 1839), p. 169.

[38]These heroes also champion the cause of young love. Metamora helps Oceana to marry her true love; Tecumseh saves Edward for the faithful Linda; Carabasset saves the white heroine from rape.

[39]In "The Argument" that precedes the play, the author says that Logan, in the tradition of his father, had been active in movements to reconcile the reds and whites until his whole family was massacred in 1774. (Some authorities disagree with this characterization. See Bernard W. Sheehan, *Seeds of Extinction* [Chapel Hill, N.C.: Univ. of North Carolina Press, 1973], p. 109.) This connection between mercy and whites is especially ironic in this play based on the actual unprovoked and brutal slaughter of all of Logan's tribe by frontiersmen.

[40]Doddridge, p. 34. This speech in its entirety was celebrated by Thomas Jefferson's *Notes on the State of Virginia* (1784). According to Pearce, p. 79, its authenticity was finally accepted, and it became a test piece in McGuffey's Fourth and Fifth readers.

[41]L.H. Medina, *Nick of the Woods in Three Acts* (Boston: William Spencer, Printer, 1838), p. 2.

[42]Washington Irving objected particularly to this stoic characterization. "Indians are by no means the stoics they are represented, unbending, without a tear or a smile. They may be grave and taciturn among strangers, but gay and even garrulous when with acquaintances. At times, there is humor and laughter; and then again tears flow in abundance at the death of a relative or friend." Keiser, p. 54.

[43]Scalping was popularized by the Spanish, French, Dutch and English Colonists. For example, Massachusetts paid twelve pounds per Indian scalp in 1703 and one hundred pounds in 1722 (Brandon, p. 310).

[44]In the preface the author cites the criticism that his Indians are not fierce enough— that they "have but little resemblance to the wild sons of the forest" (Deering, p. 3). He feels obliged to explain that the Norridgewok Indians, from whose history this play is taken, had been softened by the influence of the Jesuit who had lived with them for forty years.

[45]Herman Melville, *The Confidence Man: His Masquerade*, ed. Elizabeth Foster (New York: Hendricks House, 1954).

[46]Benjamin Spencer argues that the progressive spirit of antebellum America explains the representation of the Indians' fate as both inhumane and inevitable. Since they were "savages," there is no primitivistic nostalgia for a lost Paradise. Yet "if American common sense precluded pictures of aboriginal Edens, American justice nevertheless demanded that at least something be told... of the 'dismal tale of foul oppressions borne' ".(p. 107). *The Quest for Nationality: An American Literary Campaign* (Syracuse: Syracuse Univ. Pres, 1957), p. 107.

Chapter 4

[1]Washington Irving, *A Tour of the Prairies* (New York: R.F. Fenno & Co., 1900), p. 27.

[2]Although the fragmentation and stasis may be viewed as constant features of popular nineteenth-century literature, they figure in the characterization of Native Americans in American literature and the American imagination from the earliest accounts of explorers to contemporary westerns.

[3]Henry David Thoreau, *The Maine Woods*, ed. Dudley Lunt (New Haven, Conn.: College and University Press Publishers, 1950), p. 34.

[4]Matacoran, the rejected warrior-lover of Pocahontas in Custis' play, takes another alternative and goes West. In *The Octoroon*, it is recommended that Wah-No-Tee "return" to the West, although it is never established that he came from there. By this time (1859), Jackson's Policy of Removal had relocated many tribes in the Indian Territory in Kansas, Missouri and Oklahoma.

[5]Pearce, pp. 239-240. Later in the play, a Catholic lady refuses marriage with a

Protestant soldier because her religion forbids it. The suitor pleads, "Heaven looks upon us all with the same kind eye and will bless the virtuous of every denomination" (p. 40).

[6]Doddridge, p. 7. The doom is not only extinction by some unspecified and perhaps long-lasting passing away, but "extermination"—violent, utter and immediate destruction.

[7]Stone, p. 36. The vengeance is enacted without cause: the colonial captives are returned in good faith, but the whites release their captives, Matamora's wife and child, to a murderous mob.

[8]Lawrence J. Friedman notes that by the 1830s there was "an enormous body of material to sustain a nostalgic vision of [Washington] as a demigod-like Founding Father," characterized by flawlessness and rootedness. Friedman attributes this characterization of "the hot-headed Virginia planter" to the irreconcilable post-Revolutionary cravings for both perfection and stability. "By identifying with his mythic qualities, patriots gained a sense of personal stability and national pride" (*Inventors of the Promised Land* [New York: Knopf, 1975], pp. 47-49).

[9]Ronald N. Satz, *American Indian Policy in the Jacksonian Era* (Lincoln, NE.: Univ. of Nebraska Press, 1975), p. 2.

[10]Satz notes that virtually every American president had "seriously considered" a removal policy (p. 6).

[11]George Catlin, *Lost Rambles Amongst the Indians of the Rocky Mountains and the Andes*, ed. Marvin Ross (Norman: Univ. of Oklahoma Press, 1959), pp. 354-355.

[12]Fiedler (*Love and Death*, first edition) contends that the American gothic novel accommodated the dark American vision that resulted from the fears generated by national guilts over the treatment of dark-skinned races, and the general failure to live up to founding ideals. He says that tragedy would have been an accommodating form, had American playwrights felt secure with the classical forms.

[13]Pocahontas, of course, is the heroine, but her heroine status is qualified by her "savageness." Her greatest virtue is to recognize the superiority of the white man's religion, culture and sexual prowess.

[14]The sequence of page numbers for the fourth act of *Metamora* is violated because that act has only recently been found in the Lord Chamberlain's plays in the British Museum, and appears in the appendix at the end of the volume. Previously, the two extant copies, The Forrest Home and the University of Utah manuscripts, had, respectively, Metamora's speeches from the fourth act and a summary of the action.

Henry Wadsworth Longfellow, "Hiawatha" in *The Poetical Works of Henry Wadsworth Longfellow*, V. 11 (Boston: Houghton Mifflin, 1886), p. 280. Longfellow was confused about Indian identity as well. He mistook the historical Iroquois statesman Hiawatha for the mythic Algonquin folk hero, Manezebo.

[16]Even the women, red and white alike, apart from the convert Pocahontas, are inspired by this passion. When Jessie McDonald of Jones' *Tecumseh* saves the life of her lover-to-be, he asks how she can be repaid: "By a life preserved for the service of our country" (p. 2). Jones observed that the poet's creative effort is inspired by patriotism (Preface).

[17]Indian translators record his name as "Shooting Star."

[18]The truth was often not known and when known it was often not glorifying.

[19]The interest in origins is also indicated by numerous cases of hidden identities. There are two in *Metamora*, two in *Nick of the Woods*, two in *The Indian Princess* and one in Owen's *Pocahontas*.

[20]Richard Slotkin writes of the American effort to achieve an authoritative identity through identification with the Indian, particularly with savage power. He suggests this process had two stages: first, a submersion in the carnage against the Indian; and second, defeat and absorption of the savage.

[21]Lawrence J. Friedman notes that "public exaltation of the New Nation expanded as self-doubts heightened. It was as if outward boastings compensated for inner

apprehensions. Perhaps spread-eagle-patriots needed to proclaim the supremacies of the New Nation all the louder to quiet the feeling that the United States was no better than the corrupt mother country from which it had broken" (*Inventors of the Promised Land* [New York: Knopf, 1975], p. 2).

[22]Winthrop Jordon, "Families Politics: Thomas Paine and the Killing of the King, 1776," *The Journal of American History*, Vol. LX, No. 2, Sept. 1973.

[24]Edwin Burrows and Michael Wallace, "The American Revolution: The Ideology and Psychology of National Liberation," *Perspectives in American History*, Vol. 1, 1972, pp. 167-306.

[25]Geoffrey Gorer, *The American People, A Study in National Character* (New York: Norton, 1948).

[26]Frederic Crews, *Sins of the Fathers* (New York: Oxford Univ. Press, 1966).

[27]Francis Blake, "An Oration Pronounced at Worcester [Massachusetts]" on July 4, 1912 (Worcester, Ma.: 1812). Quoted in Nagel, p. 9.

[28]The early reviews of *Metamora* suggest that Walter, the American prototype, was actually the son of the despicable aristocrat Fitzarnold. If so, the love triangle involved father and son. The Freudian implications are obvious. Two extant copies of *Metamora*, The Forrest Home and the University of Utah manuscripts, however, show that Walter has a loving parent, Sir Arthur Vaughn, from whom he has been separated.

[29]This is not true of the heroine, Pocahontas. She defies her father and deserts her countrymen, although she is sometimes represented as true to higher causes, i.e., Christianity and American destiny.

[30]Berkhofer notes that the basic premises about the Indian and his fate remain the same from the captivity narrative to contemporary westerns: they are "indelibly engraved on the white mind." He reasons that the consistency suggests that the American conscience still needs to be reassured about the rightness of the past: that "the destruction of Native American cultures and the expropriation of Native American lands still demand justification in White American eyes" (p. 104).

[31]Bernard W. Sheehan argues that American thinkers and policymakers of the late eighteenth and early nineteenth centuries conceived of the Indian as a noble savage, readily convertible to civilized ways. The philanthrophy based on these assumptions, he argues, helped destroy Indian integrity (*Seeds of Extinction: Jeffersonian Philanthropy and the American Indian* [Chapel Hill: Univ. of North Carolina Press, 1973]). Michal Rogin challenges this view in "Indian Extinction, American Regeneration," *Journal of Ethnic Studies*, II, Spring 1974, pp. 93-104.

[32]Although miscegenation was common on the frontier, it is non-existent in the non-Pocahontas plays.

[33]Although the artistry of these playwrights is negligible, the existence of this subsurface concern calls to mind Lawrence's assertion that "this quality of duplicity... is almost inevitable in an American book. The author is unconscious of it himself. He is sincere in his own intention. And yet, all the time, the artist, who writes as a somnambulist, in the spell of pure truth as in a dream, is contravened and contradicted by the wakeful man and moralist who sits at the desk." See *The Symbolic Meaning* (New York: Viking Press, 1964), p. 18.

[34]Berkhofer sees the ambivalence of the whites' Indian imagery as a reflection of their conflicting evaluation of their own society and culture (p. 27).

Chapter 5

[1]Page Smith, "Anxiety and Despair in American History," *William and Mary Quarterly*, XXVI, July 1969, p. 417.

[2]Ralph Waldo Emerson, "Lectures on the Times," in *The Dial* (Boston), III, Oct. 1842, p. 194.

[3]John Winthrop, "The Humble Request of Massachusetts Puritans and a Modell of Christian Charity," ed. S.E. Morrison (Boston: Old South Association, 1916), p. 16.

[4]David H. Fischer, *The Revolution of American Conservatism* (New York: Harper & Bros., 1965).

[5]Charles Eliot Norton, ed., *Letters of James Russell Lowell* (New York: Harper & Bros., 1894), p. 134.

[6]Harry Warfel, *Noah Webster, Schoolmaster to America* (New York: Macmillan, 1936), p. 432.

[7]Henry David Thoreau, *Walden or Life in the Woods*, afterword by Perry Miller (New York: New American Library, 1960), p. 67.

[8]H. Richard Niebuhr, *The Responsible Self: An Essay in Christian Moral Philosophy* (New York: Scribner's, 1963), p. 151-152.

[9]Quentin Anderson suggests that there has never been a strong source of institutionalized reality in the United States because authority has always been suspect among a people whose nation was founded through the defiance of authority and refusal of traditional duty.

[10]From Lawrence Friedman's point of view, the self-doubts and apprehensiveness of post-revolutionary America was due to the conflict of two internal cravings: the desire for national perfection and a flawless America; and the desire for stability, a sense of place and order. These desires were irreconcilable "because the first demands motion and a spirit of restless discontent with things as they are... [and the other] a sense of personal stability, place and order" (p. 43).

[11]*Adams-Jefferson Correspondence*, II (Chapel Hill: Univ. of North Carolina Press, 1959), p. 20.

[12]Calvin Colton, ed., *The Life, Correspondence, and Speeches of Henry Clay*. VI (New York, 1864), pp. 367-368.

[13]Roy P. Basler, ed., *The Collected Works of Abraham Lincoln,* I (New Brunswick: Rutgers University Press, 1953), p. 108.

[14]Ralph Rusk, ed., *The Letters of Ralph Waldo Emerson* (New York: Columbia Univ. Press, 1939), p. 274.

[15]The New World was also characterized as the place of the underworld or afterworld, the world below consciousness, the kingdom of dreams, and the realm of Moira (Slotkin, p. 28). This duality implies recognition of the casual relationship between freedom and terror.

[16]Leo Marx in *The Machine in the Garden* (New York: Oxford Univ. Press, 1964) points out that the pastoral ideal continues to exercise control of the native imagination as the meaning of America.

[17]Charles Burr Todd, *Life and Letters of Joel Barlow, L.L.D.* (New York: Putnam's Sons, 1886), p. 207. (Henry Thoreau would have "capitalized" on the opportunities for economic puns in *deposit* and *interest*.)

[18]Calvin Colton, ed., *The Private Correspondence of Henry Clay* (Cincinnati: A.S. Barnes & Co., 1856), p. 498.

[19]James Fenimore Cooper, *Home As Found* in *The Choice Works of Cooper,* XIV (New York: W.A. Townsend, 1856), p. 19.

[20]John H. Rice, "The Power of Love," *The National Preacher,* III (Oct. 1828), p. 65.

[21]A writer named George W. Bethune, who believed that America's meaning lay in her "peculiar" relation with God, reasoned that "Jesus Christ was a patriot," and therefore, "every Christian should be a patriot." *Our Liberties: Their Danger* (Philadelphia: N.P., 1835), pp. 5-6.

[22]James D. Richardson, ed., *A Compilation of the Messages and Papers of the Presidents,* I (New York, 1897), p. 258.

[23]Joseph Campbell defines myth as "traditional metaphor addressed to ultimate questions."

[24]Quentin Anderson attributes the loss of energetic belief to the explicitness of the

national compact with religion and the explicitness of rational religion itself.

[25]William Ellery Channing, in "Christian Examiner," V (March and April 1828), p. 143. Quoted in Anderson, p. 29.

[26]Leslie Fiedler, *Love and Death in the American Novel*, Revised Edition (New York: Stein and Day, 1966), p. 81. Fiedler argues that this asexual, spiritual conception of women, along with other factors, led to the search in our fiction for an innocent substitute for marriage and a failure to deal maturely with any form of adult heterosexuality.

[27]*Love and Death*, First Edition, p. xviii.

[28]*Ibid.*, p. xxix. These reversals pertained to the conception of the Native American as well, at least among the intelligentsia. In 1843, Margaret Fuller, who had traveled among the Indians, declared that the Indians had more instinctive existence and a more integrated life than the whites: Civilization might have a larger mind, but the result was a less perfect nature. Fuller, *Writings*, ed. Mason Wade (New York: Viking, 1941), pp. 57-58. After an Indian-guided tour of Maine, Thoreau wrote to H.G. Otis Blake in 1857 that his association with his guide had expanded his understanding of the world. "The Indian begins where we leave off.... I rejoice to find that intelligence flows in other channels than I knew...." F.B. Sandborn, ed., *Familiar Letters of Henry David Thoreau* (Boston: Houghton Mifflin, 1894), pp. 369-370.

[29]*Walden*, p. 12.

[30]*Love and Death*, First Edition, pp. xxxii-xxxiii.

[31]**Henry James, Sr., "Democracy and Its Issues,"** *Lectures and Miscellaneous* **(New York: Redfield, 1852).**

[32]Alexis de Toqueville noted in 1837 that "among democratic nations, each generation is a new people." *Democracy in America*, trans. George Lawrence (New York: Harper & Row, 1966), p. 676.

[33]Ralph Waldo Emerson, *Journals*, Vol. 4 (Cambridge, Mass.: Riverside Press, 1910-1914), p. 495. Geoffrey Gorer, like Anderson, argues that all American history is characterized by a repulsion for authority. He views the divided structure of the federal government—the separation of powers and the system of checks and balances—as an effort to erect inseparable legal barriers to the excessive authority of one person or group. The "Just So" story (Freud) is used to imagine the founding of America: downtrodden sons combine to kill the tyrannical father. Afterwards, overwhelmed by the crime and fearful that one will attempt to take the murdered father's place, they make a compact which establishes the legal equality of the brothers, based on a common renunciation of the father's authority and privilege. *The American People* (New York: Norton, 1948), p. 29.

[34]Michael Paul Rogin argues that American authority was achieved through the dispossession and destruction of our "red children." His argument is considered in more detail later in this chapter.

[35]Samuel L. Knapp, *An Address* (Boston, 1826), p. 26.

[36]There was filiopiety in Daniel Webster's 1814 proposal that no one be allowed to vote until he was 45 or to hold office until he was 50 (Nagel, p. 35).

[37]*The American Review of History and Politics* I, **(Philadelphia, 1811), 87.**

[38]*Brownson's Quarterly Review*, I (1944), p. 493.

[39]Lawrence Cremin, ed., *The Republic and the School* (New York, Columbia Teachers' College Press, 1957), p. 100.

[40]*Hakluytus Posthumus, or Purchas His Pilgrims*, ed. Samuel Purchas (Glasgow, 1906), **xix, 218-265. Quoted in Pearce, p. 7.**

[41]Winthrop to Sir Nathaniel Rich, May 22, 1634. *Winthrop Papers*, III (Boston: Massachusetts Historical Society, 1943), p. 167. Quoted in Pearce, p. 19.

[42]Obviously, Manifest Destiny also provided a rationalization for the ruthless and fraudulent expropriation of Indian land and minerals and for the genocidal warfare. The Big Horn Association, a mining organization that wanted to trespass on the Sioux treaty land, claimed in typical fashion, divine justification for their proposals: "The rich and beautiful valleys of Wyoming are destined for the occupancy and sustenance of the Anglo-

Saxon race. The wealth that for untold ages has lain beneath the snow-capped summits of our mountains has been placed there by Providence to reward the brave spirits whose lot it is to compose the advance-guard of civilization. The Indian must stand aside or be overwhelmed by the ever-advancing and ever-increasing tide of emigration. The destiny of the aborigines is written in characters not to be mistaken. The same inscrutable Arbiter that decreed the downfall of Rome has pronounced the doom of extinction upon the red men of America." *Cheyenne Wyoming Daily Leader*, March 3, 1870. Quoted by Dee Brown in *Bury My Heart At Wounded Knee*, p. 189.

⁴³Timothy Flint, *Indian Wars of the West, containing Biographical Sketches of Those Pioneers who Headed the Western Settlers in Repelling the Attacks of the Savages* (Cincinnati: E.H. Fleet, 1833), pp. 36-37.

⁴⁴In *The American Condition* (Garden City, N.Y.: Doubleday, 1974), p. 9, Richard N. Goodwin writes about modern life in America: "Individualism has led in our time to the destruction of those social bonds through which individuals could express and exercise authority over the conditions of social life. This leads to the dissolution of community, shared social consciousness, and moral authority, finding ourselves amid a fragmentation so complete that the isolated individual, man alone, is driven to seek new authority, a binding force made more coercive because, lacking inward roots, it must be imposed."

⁴⁵Michael Paul Rogin argues that Andrew Jackson's remarkable popularity was due to his infusion of American politics with "a regenerated paternal authority" (p. 15), a need generated by the collapse of traditional forms of authority.

⁴⁶*The Complete Works of Ralph Waldo Emerson* Vol. 1, Intro. by Edward Waldo Emerson (Boston: Houghton Mifflin, 1903), pp 114-115.

⁴⁷*The Works of Ralph Waldo Emerson*, Vol 1 (Boston: Jefferson Press, n.d.), p. 55.

⁴⁸Lawrence Friedman notes that in a "patriotic crusade" to create a national identity, a kind of mythic quest, writers by the 1830s had invented a mythic Founding Father, an apotheosized George Washington (pp. 45-47).

⁴⁹Richard Poirier, in *A World Elsewhere* (New York: Oxford Univ. Press, 1966), remarks on the obsession of American writers, from Cooper to Mailer, with the "invention in language of environments that permit unhampered freedom of consciousness" (p. 8), worlds free from the usual economic, social and biological realities. This indicates a lack of faith in the usual historical forces to produce genuine freedom of consciousness, a conclusion that is evident in the anxiety about American destiny and responsibility during that period. It also suggests that American authors need to create imaginary environments for their heroes to realize other impossible American dreams.

⁵⁰My discussion of the materials for a native literature is based on Roderick Nash's *Wilderness and the American Mind* (New Haven: Yale Univ. Press, 1967), and William Ellery Sedgwick's "The Materials for an American Literature," *Harvard Studies and Notes in Philology and Literature,"* XVII (1935), pp. 141-162.

⁵¹*The American Monthly Magazine*, I (1819), p. 389.

⁵²Edwin S. Fussell points out that Henry Thoreau's Indian notebooks, principally derivative material from widely varied sources, recorded over fourteen years, were probably preparatory to writing an ancient history of America: Fussell writes: "Thoreau could easily [have] arm[ed] them with an ancient world more primitive, more mythical, more 'shadowy and unreal' than anything the upstart Europeans could boast.... The Indian Thoreau said, 'lives three thousand years deep into time, an age not yet described by poets,' by implication permitting himself to antedate even his favorite Homer." "The Red Face of Man," *Thoreau: A Collection of Essays*, ed. Sherman Paul (Englewood Cliffs, N.J.: Prentice-Hall, 1962), p. 146.

⁵³Dr. Walter Channing, "Literary Delinquency in America," *The North American Review*, II (1815), p. 39.

⁵⁴James A. Hillhouse, "On some of the Considerations which should Influence an Epic or a Tragic Writer" in *Dramas, Discourses, and other Pieces* (Boston: Little, Brown,

1839), p. 7.

⁵⁵*The Port Folio*, VII (1819), p. 26.

⁵⁶James Fenimore Cooper, *Notions of the Americans*, II (New York: Stringer and Townsend, 1828), pp. 242-243.

⁵⁷John Bristed, *America and Her Resources* (London: H. Colburn, 1818), pp. 355-356.

⁵⁸Washington Irving, "A Biographical Sketch of Thomas Campbell," *Biographies and Miscellanies* (New York: Putnam, 1869), p. 132. Quoted in Sedgwick, p. 160.

⁵⁹P.M. Marsh, ed., *Prose of Freneau* (Metuchen, N.J.: Scarecrow Press, 1955), p. 228. Quoted in Nash, p. 68.

⁶⁰Philip Rahv, ed., *Discovery of Europe: The Story of American Experience in the Old World* (Boston: Houghton Mifflin, 1947), p. 52; in Nash, p. 69.

⁶¹Samuel Williams, *The Natural and Civil History of Vermont*, 2nd rev. ed., 2 vols. (Burlington: Samuel Mills, 1809), I, p. 159; in Nash, p. 68.

In a letter from Thomas Jefferson to Marquis de Chastellux dated July 7, 1785, Jefferson says that it has been reported that Paris is more humid than Philadelphia and that American humidity is generally superior. He comments that some believe that this causes animals to be larger here, but that he himself is doubtful. Julian P. Boyd, ed., *The Papers of Thomas Jefferson*, Vol. VIII (Princeton: Princeton Univ. Press, 1953), pp. 184-186.

⁶²Estwick Evans, *A Pedestrian's Tour of Four Thousand Miles through the Western States and Territories during the Winter and Spring of 1818* (Concord, N.H.: Spear, 1819), p. 102.

⁶³Washington Irving, despite his description of Indians as subjects "worthy of... romantic fiction," never used them himself as material for fiction. However, he wrote two essays, "Indian Traits" and "Phillip of Pokonoket," which were incorporated in *The Sketch Book*, and three other works—*A Tour of the Prairies*, 1835; *Astoria*, 1836: and *The Adventures of Captain Bonneville*, 1837—in which Indians play a major role. The first of these is autobiographical, concerning Irving's Western trip of 1832; the second and third are based on the diaries and reports of travellers, hunters and trappers in Indian country. In all three, the Indian is generally viewed as an admirable and heroic defender of his homeland against the ruthless invaders.

⁶⁴Cooper, *The Deerslayer*, p. 38.

⁶⁵*United States Literary Gazette* (March 1826), III, p. 456.

⁶⁶*The North American Review*, XXIII (1826), p. 166.

⁶⁷"Domestic Literature," *The Atlantic Magazine*, I (1824), p. 130; in Sedgwick, p. 150.

⁶⁸Benjamin Spencer argues that there was an "all but inevitable" tendency among cisatlantic, ante-bellum writers to subsume the Indian under Old World modes, particularly the Homeric (p. 164).

⁶⁹William Tudor, "An Address," *The North American Review*, II (1815), pp. 14-29; in Sedgwick, p. 149.

⁷⁰Bernard Sheehan argues that American thinkers believed that the differences between Indians and Anglo-Europeans were caused by environmental differences merely and that the Indian could be brought to civilization readily. In Sheehan's view this conception led to the philanthropic reform or conversion policies of the early nineteenth century which destroyed the integrity of Indian cultures but failed to convert them to Anglo-Europeans culture. He believes this was done without malice by the philanthropists who were the instruments of American Indian policy. This view seems simplistic, given the evidence of a widespread ante-bellum awareness of the devastating effects of such policies.

Appendix

Indian Dramas Included in this Study

The Indian Princess or La Belle Sauvage (1808), by J.N. Barker.

Oolaita, An Indian Heroine (1821), by Lewis Deffebach.

Logan, Last of the Race of Skikellemus, Chief of the Cayuga Nation (1821), by Joseph Doddridge.

Pocahontas or the Settlers of Virginia (1827), by George Washington Parke Custis.

Metamora or the Last of the Wampanoags (1829), by John A. Stone.

Carabasset (1830), by Nathaniel Deering.

Pontiac or the Siege of Detroit (1835), by General Alexander Macomb.

Tecumseh or The Battle of the Thames (1836), by William Emmons.

Pocahontas: A Historical Drama (1937), by Robert Dale Owen.

Nick of the Woods (1838), by Miss Louisa H. Medina.

The Forest Princess or Two Centuries Ago (1844), by Charlotte M.S. Barnes.

Tecumseh and the Prophet of the West: An Original Historical Israel-Indian Tragedy (1844), by George Jones.

Pocahontas or the Gentle Savage (1859), by John Brougham.

The Octoroon or Life in Louisiana (1859), by Dion Boucicault.

Bibliography

Adams-Jefferson Correspondence. II. Chapel Hill: University of North Carolina Press, 1959.

The American Monthly Magazine, I, 1828, 389.

The American Review of History and Politics. I, Philadelphia, 1811.

Anderson, Quentin. *The Imperial Self: An Essay in American Literary and Cultural History.* New York: Alfred A. Knopf, 1971.

Armstrong, Virginia and Turner, Frederick III, eds. *I Have Spoken.* Chicago: Swallow Press, 1971.

The Atlantic Magazine. I, 1824, 19.

Barbour, Philip L. *The Three Worlds of Captain John Smith.* Boston: Houghton Mifflin, 1964.

Barker, J.N. *The Indian Princess or La Belle Sauvage.* Philadelphia: T.G. Palmer, Printers, 1808.

Barnes, Charlotte. *The Forest Princess or Two Centuries Ago* from *Play, Prose, and Poetry,* by Charlotte M.S. Barnes. Philadelphia: E.H. Butler & Co., 1848.

Berkhofer, Robert F., Jr. *The White Man's Indian: Images of the American Indian from Columbus to the Present.* New York: Knopf, 1978.

Bethune, George W. *Our Liberties: Their Danger.* Philadelphia: N.P., 1835.

Bodkin, Maude. *Archetypal Patterns in Poetry.* London: Oxford University Press, 1963.

Boucicault, Dion. *The Octoroon or Life in Louisiana.* New York: Samuel French and Son, 1859.

Boyd, Julian P., ed. *The Papers of Thomas Jefferson.* Vol. VIII. Princeton: Princeton University Press, 1953.

Brackenridge, Henry. *Indian Atrocities: Narratives of the Perils and Suffering of Dr. Knight and John Slover Among the Indians During the Revolutionary War.* Cincinnati, Ohio: N.P., 1867.

Brandon, William, *The American Heritage Book of Indians.* New York: American Heritage Publishing Co., 1961.

Bristed, John. *America and Her Resources.* London: H. Colburn, 1818.

Brougham, John. *Pocahontas or The Gentle Savage* New York: Samuel French, 1859.

Brown, Dee. *Bury My Heart at Wounded Knee.* New York: Holt, Rinehart, & Winston, 1970.

Brownson's Quarterly Review. I, 1844.

Buntin, Arthur Roy. "The Indian in American Literature, 1680-1760." Diss. Univ. of Washington, 1961.

Burrows, Edwin and Wallace, Michael. "The American Revolution: The Ideology and Psychology of National Liberation." *Perspectives in American History,* VI, 1972.

Cahn, Edgar S., ed. *Our Brother's Keeper: The Indian in White America.* New York: A New Community Press Book, 1970.

Campbell, Joseph. *The Hero With a Thousand Faces.* New York: World, Meridian Books, 1949.

Campbell, Joseph. *Myths to Live By.* New York: Viking, 1972.

Catlin, George. *Lost Rambles Amongst the Indians of the Rocky Mountains and the Andes.* ed. Marvin Ross. Norman: University of Oklahoma Press, 1959.

Channing, Dr. Walter. "Literary Delinquency in America." *The North American Review,* II, 1815, 3.

Collier, John. *Indians of the Americas: The Long Hope.* New York: New American Library, 1947.

Colton, Calvin, ed. *The Life, Correspondence and Speeches of Henry Clay,* VI. New York, 1864.

Conrad, Joseph. *The Heart of Darkness.* ed. Bruce Harkness. San Francisco: Wadsworth, 1960.

Cooper, James Fenimore. *Home as Found* in *The Choice Works of Cooper.* Vol. XILV. New York: W.A. Townsend, 1856.

————. *Notions of the Americans.* Vol. II. New York: Stringer and Townsend, 1828.

————. *The Deerslayer.* New York: The New American Library, A Signet Classic, 1963.

Cremin, Laurence, ed. *The Republic and the School.* New York: Columbia Teachers' College Press, 1957.

Crews, Frederick. *Sins of the Fathers.* New York: Oxford Univ. Press, 1966.

Custis, George Washington Parke. *Pocahontas or The Settlers of Virginia.* Philadelphia: N.P., 1827.

Debo, Angie. *A History of the Indians of the United States.* Norman: Univ. of Oklahoma Press, 1970.

deCrevecoeur, G.J. *Letters from an American Farmer.* New York: Suton, 1943.

Deering, Nathaniel. *Carabasset: A Tragedy in Five Acts.* Portland, ME.: S. Colman, Printer, 1830.

Deffebach, Lewis. *Oolaita, An Indian Heroine.* Philadelphia: N.P., 1821.

deNagy, Niclas Christoph. *Ezra Pound's Poetics and Literary Tradition: The Critical Decade.* Basel, Switzerland: Franche Verlag Bern, 1966.

deToqueville, Alexis. *Democracy in America.* trans. George Lawrence. New York: Harper & Row, 1966.

Dobyns, Henry F. "Estimating Aboriginal American Population: An Appraisal of Techniques with a New Hemispheric Estimate." *Current Anthropology,* Oct. 1966, Vol. 7, No. 4.

Doddridge, Joseph. *Logan, The Last of the Race of Skikellemus, Chief of the Cayuga Nation.* Buffalo Creeks, VA.: N.P., 1823.

Donaldson, Thomas. 'The George Catlin Indian Gallery." Smithsonian Institution, *Annual Report,* V, 505.

Drake, Samuel G. *The History of the Indian Wars in New England.* New York: B. Franklin, 1971.

Ellis, Edward S. *The History of Our Country.* Indianapolis: N.P., 1900.

Emerson, Ralph Waldo. "Lectures on the Times." *The Dial* (Boston) III, Oct. 1842, 194.

————. *Journals.* Vol. 4. Cambridge, MA.: Riverside Press, 1909-1914.

————. *The Complete Works of Ralph Waldo Emerson.* Vol. I. Introduction by Edward Waldo Emerson. Boston: Houghton Mifflin, 1903.

————. The Works of Ralph Waldo Emerson. Vol. I. Boston: The Jefferson Press, N.D.

Emmons, William. *Tecumseh or The Battle of the Thames.* Philadelphia: N.P., 1836.

Fey, Harold E. and McNickle, D'Arcy. *Indians and Other Americans: Two Ways of Life Meet.* New York: Harper & Row, 1970.

Fiedler, Leslie. *Love and Death in the American Novel.* New York: Stein and Day, 1960.

————. *Love and Death in the American Novel.* Rev. Ed. New York: Stein and Day, 1966.

Fischer, David N. *The Revolution of American Conservatism.* New York: Harper & Bros., 1965.

Flint, Timothy. *Indian Wars of the West. Containing Biographical Sketches of Those Pioneers Who Headed the Western Settlers in Repelling the Attacks of the Savages,* Cincinnati, OH: E.H. Fleet, 1833.

Forbes, Jack D. *The Indian in America's Past.* Englewood Cliffs, N.J.: Prentice-Hall, 1964.

Force, Peter, ed., *Forces Tracts and Other Papers Relating Principally to the Origin, Settlement and Progress of the Colonies in North America, from the Discovery of the Country to the Year 1776.* 2, No. 5 (1835).

Friedman, Lawrence J. *Inventors of the Promised Land.* New York: Knopf, 1975.

Frye, Northrop. *Anatomy of Criticism.* New York: Atheneum, 1966.

Fuller, Margaret. *Writings,* ed. Mason Wade. New York: Viking Press, 1941.

Fussell, Edwin S. "The Red Face of Man," in *Thoreau: A Collection of Essays.* ed. Sherman Paul, Englewood Cliffs, N.J.: Prentice-Hall, 1962.

Goodwin, Richard H. *The American Condition,* Garden City, N.J.: Doubleday 1974.

Gorer, Geoffrey. *The American People, a Study in National Character.* New York: Norton, 1948.

Grossman, James. *James Fenimore Cooper.* New York: William Sloan Associates, 1949.

Hawthorne, Nathaniel. *The Marble Faun or The Romance of Monte Beni.* New York: New American Library, A Signet Classic, 1961.

Heckewelder, John. *Account of the History, Manners, and Customs of the Indian Nations, Who Once Inhabited Pennsylvania and the Neighboring States.* Philadelphia: American Philosophical Society, 1819.

Heller, Eric. *The Works of Nietzsche.* Tape, Casette Curriculum, Everett Edwards, Inc.

Hertzberg, Hazel W. *The Search for an American Indian Identity: Modern Pan-Indian Movements.* Syracuse, N.Y.: 1971.

Howard, Helen Addison. *War Chief Joseph.* Caldwell, Idaho: Caxton Printers, Ltd., 1941.

Huizinga, John. *Homo Ludens.* Boston: Beacon Press, 1955.

Irving, Washington. *A Tour of the Prairies.* New York: R.F. Fenno & Co.,1900.

————. *A Tour of the Prairies,* ed. John Francis McDermott. Norman: Univ. of Oklahoma Press, 1956.

————. *The Adventures of Captain Bonneville*. New York: Putnam's, 1854.

————. *The Sketch Book*. Philadelphia: Lea & Blanchard, 1839.

Jackson, Donald, ed. *Letters of the Lewis and Clark Expedition*. Urbana: Univ. of Illinois Press, 1962.

Jane, Cecil, trans. *The Journal of Christopher Columbus*. New York: Clark N. Potter, 1960.

Jennings, Frances. *The Invasion of America: Indians, Colonialism, and the Cant of Conquest*. Chapel Hill: Univ. of North Carolina Press, 1975.

Jones, George. *Tecumseh and the Prophet of the West, an Original Historical Israel-Indian Tragedy*. New York: Harper & Bros., 1844.

Jordan, Winthrop. "Familial Politics: Thomas Paine and the Killing of the **King, 1776."** *The Journal of American History,* Vol. 1, LX, No. 2, Sept. 1973.

Keiser, Albert. *The Indian in American Literature*. New York: Oxford Univ. Press, 1933.

Kopit, Arthur. *Indians*. New York: Bantam Books, 1971.

Lanman, C. *Summer in the Wilderness*. New York: D. Appleton & Co., 1847.

Lawrence, D.H. *Studies in Classic American Literature*. New York: Seltzer, 1923.

————. *The Symbolic Meaning*. New York: Viking, 1964.

Leonard, Elizabeth Jane and Goodman, Julia Cody. *Buffalo Bill: King of the Old West*. New York: Library Publishers, 1955.

Lewis, R.W.B. *The American Adam: Innocence, Tragedy and Tradition in the Nineteenth Century*. Chicago: Univ. of Chicago Press, 1964.

Longfellow, Henry Wadsworth. "Hiawatha" in *The Poetical Works of Henry Wadsworth Longfellow*. Boston: Houghton Mifflin, 1886.

Macomb, General Alexander. *Pontiac or The Siege of Detroit: A Drama in Three Acts*. Boston: S. Colman, Printer, 1835.

Marx, Leo. *The Machine in the Garden*. New York. Oxford Univ. Press, 1964.

Mather, Increase. *A Brief History of War with the Indians in New England*. London: Printed for Richard Chiswel, 1676.

Medina, L.H. *Nick of the Woods in Three Acts*. Boston: William Spencer, Printer,1838.

Melville, Herman. *The Confidence Man: His Masquerade*. ed. Elizabeth Foster. New York: Hendricks House, 1954.

————. *Moby Dick or The Whale*. ed. Luther Mansfield. New York: Hendricks House, 1952.

Merton, Thomas. *Conjectures of a Guilty Bystander*. New York: Doubleday, 1965.

Meserve, Walter. *An Outline History of American Drama*. Totowa, N.J.: Littlefield, Adams & Co., 1965.

Miller, Perry. *Errand Into the Wilderness.* Cambridge: Harvard Univ. Press, 1956.

————. ed. *The Complete Writings of Roger Williams*. VII. New York: Russell & Russell, 1963.

Moses, Montrose. *Representative Plays by American Dramatists*. New York: Benjamin Blom, Inc., 1948.

————. *The American Dramatist*. Boston: Little, Brown, 1911.

Nagel, Paul C. *This Sacred Trust: American Nationality, 1798-1898*. New York:

Oxford Univ. Press, 1971.

Nash, Gary B. "The Image of the Indian in the Southern Colonial Mind." *William & Mary Quarterly*, April 1972, Vol. 29, No. 2.

Nash, Roderick. *Wilderness and the American Mind*. New Haven: Yale Univ. Press, 1967.

The New Englander, IV, July 1846, 381.

Niebuhr, H. Richard. *The Responsible Self: An Essay in Christian Moral Philosophy*. New York: Scribners, 1963.

The North American Review, XXIII, 1826, 166.

Norton, Charles Eliot, ed. *Letters of James Russell Lowell*, I. New York: Harper & Bros., 1894.

Novak, Michael. *The Experience of Nothingness*. New York: Harper & Row, 1970.

Nye, Russel B. *This Almost Chosen People: Essays in the History of American Ideas*. East Lansing: Michigan State Univ. Press, 1966.

Owen, Robert Dale. *Pocahontas: A Historical Drama*. New York: George Dearborn Pub., 1837.

Paulding, James Kirke. *Letters from the South*. New York: Harper & Bros., 1817.

Pearce, Roy Harvey. *The Savages of America: A Study of the Indian and the Idea of Civilization*. Baltimore: Johns Hopkins Univ. Press, 1965.

Poirier, Richard. *A World Elsewhere*. New York: Oxford Univ. Press, 1966.

The Port Folio, VII, 1819, 26.

Quinn, Arthur Hobson. *A History of American Drama*. New York: Harper & Bros., 1923.

————. *A History of the American Drama*. New York: F.S. Crofts, 1943.

————. *Representative American Plays*. New York: Century, 1917.

Rice, John H. "The Power of Love," in *The National Preacher*, III, Oct. 1828, 65.

Richardson, J.D., ed. *A Compilation of the Messages and Papers of the Presidents, 1789-1897*. Vol. II. Washington: U.S. Gov. Printing Office, N.D.

Rogin, Michael Paul. *Fathers and Children: Andrew Jackson and the Subjugation of the American Indian*. New York: Knopf, 1975.

————. "Indian Extinction, American Regeneration." *Journal of Ethnic Studies*, II, Spring 1974.

Rusk, Ralph, ed. *The Letters of Ralph Waldo Emerson*. New York: Columbia Univ. Press, 1939.

Sandborn, F.B., ed. *Familiar Letters of Henry David Thoreau*. Boston: Houghton Mifflin, 1894.

Sandoz, Mari. *Cheyenne Autumn*. New York: Discus Books, 1964.

Satz, Ronald N. *American Indian Policy in the Jacksonian Era*. Lincoln: Univ. of Nebraska Press, 1975.

Sedgwick, William Ellery. "The Materials for an American Literature." *Harvard Studies and Notes in Philology and Literature*, XVII, 1935, 141-162.

Sheehan, Bernard W. *Seeds of Extinction: Jeffersonian Philanthropy and the American Indian*. Chapel Hill: Univ. of North Carolina Press, 1973.

Slotkin, Richard. *Regeneration Through Violence, the Mythology of the American Frontier, 1600-1860*. Middletown, Conn.: Wesleyan Univ. Press, 1973.

Smith, Page. "Anxiety and Despair in American History." *William and Mary*

Quarterly, XXVI, July 1969, 417.

Spencer, Benjamin. *The Quest for Nationality: An American Literary Campaign.* Syracuse: Syracuse Univ. Press, 1957.

Stone, John A. *Metamora or The Last of the Wampanoags.* New York: N.P., 1829.

Thoreau, Henry David. *The Maine Woods.* ed. Dudley Lunt. New Haven: College and University Press Publishers, 1950.

————. *Walden: Or Life in the Woods.* Afterword by Perry Miller. New York: New American Library, 1960.

Todd, Charles Burr. *Life and Letters of Joel Barlow, L.L.D.* New York: Putnam's Sons, 1886.

Trigger, Bruce. "Ethnohistory," XXII, 1975.

Tyrell, J.B. ed. *David Thompson's Narrative of His Explorations in Western America, 1784-1812.* Toronto, Canada: Champlain Society, 1961.

United States Literary Gazette, III, March 1826, 456.

Van der Beets, Richard, ed. *Held Captive by Indians: Selected Narratives, 1642-1836.* Knoxville: Univ. of Tennessee Press, 1973.

Van Doren, Carl, ed. *Benjamin Franklin's Autobiographical Writings.* New York: Viking, 1945.

Vestal, Stanley. *Warpath and the Council Fire.* New York: Random House, 1948.

Vogel, Virgil. *This Land Was Ours.* New York: Harper & Row, 1967.

Ware, Ralph H. and Schoenberger, H.W. *America's Lost Plays.* Vols. 13-14. Bloomington: Indiana Univ. Press, 1940.

Washburn, Wilcomb E., ed. *The Indian and the Whiteman.* Garden City, N.Y.: Doubleday, 1964.

Waters, Frank. *The Man Who Killed the Deer.* Flagstaff, Ariz: Northland Press, 1942.

Williams, William Carlos. *In The American Grain.* New York: New Directions Paperbook, 1956.

Winthrop, John. "The Humble Request of Massachusetts Puritans and a Modell of Christian Charity." Ed. S.E. Morrison. Boston: Old South Assoc., 1916.

Index